HOW TO LIVE LIKE A LORD

Without Really Trying

How to Live Like a Lord

Without Really Trying

A Confidential Manual Prepared as
Part of a Survival Kit for Americans
Living in Britain, Showing How to
Get Rich in England, How to Rise
Quickly and Easily to the Top of British
Society, Examining the Blessings,
Foibles, and Weaknesses of British Life,
Providing the Reader With His Just
Share of Wealth, Warmth, Wisdom,
and Lasting Happiness, and Containing
the Thrilling Human Story of a Brave
Family's Battle Against the Elements

by Shepherd Mead
Illustrations by Anton

Bodleian Library
UNIVERSITY OF OXFORD

This edition first published in 2012 by the Bodleian Library
Broad Street
Oxford OX1 3BG

www.bodleianbookshop.co.uk

ISBN: 978 1 85124 279 5

First published in Great Britain in 1964 by Macdonald and Company
(Publishers) Ltd.

Cover design by Dot Little
Designed by Dot Little. Typeset in 11/14 pt Monotype Ehrhardt
Printed and Bound in Great Britain by TJ International Ltd, Padstow,
Cornwall on 80gsm Premium Munken Cream

British Library Catalogue in Publishing Data
A CIP record of this publication is available from the British Library

This is not *a U.S. Government Publication*

THIS BOOK is printed at private expense. Do not confuse it with publications distributed by the U.S. Government to each of the thousands of official visitors who are sent annually to Britain, to help point the British toward a better way of life.

This volume is not intended to replace the official booklets, but to supplement them, and especially to help those other thousands of non-official Americans, coming on private missions to aid the British, on a live-in basis. These lonely little bands, often just a family, are equally anxious to help the British to a better way of life, and indeed, to help themselves to as much of it as possible.

The official government visitors have been sent to guide the British, as a helmsman steers a boat, from the rear. It will be up to you, the unofficial emissaries, to lead them, from the front. Show them how easy it is to rise, so to speak, through the milk and into the cream of British society. In short, how to live like a Lord.

A Note to British Readers

THIS BOOK is intended only to show lost and bewildered Americans how to get around the British, in a nice way.

Extremists feel that for you, as Britons, to use these methods against each other would not only be unfair, but could lead to chaos, and the destruction of British society. They feel that right-thinking people should close ranks against it.

Some British readers, tossing caution to the winds, are sure to benefit extravagantly from it. Others, alas, will mistrust the easily won leisure, position and riches, and will want to return to their familiar ways of hardship, poverty, and suffering.

It is a choice you will have to make.

*   *   *   *

As in our previous text books, the bits of dialogue are intended not to amuse, but only to illustrate difficult points. The drawings and frank diagrams are included to help chart a course through what might otherwise be a formidable sea of words.

Contents

Countless "Lords" live more wretchedly than your poorest relations.

1

"Do I WANT to Live Like a Lord?"

ACTUALLY, of course, you do not. Our title refers to "living like a Lord" only because of alliteration and literary pretension.

Very few Americans would like to live like a mere "lord", a loose term which covers a frequently tatterdemalion band of marquesses, earls, viscounts, and barons, numbering nearly a thousand. Many "lords" are impoverished, some run restaurants, sell cars, play pianos, or otherwise grub for a living. Countless "lords" live more wretchedly than your poorest relations in the States, or perhaps your plumber or handyman, shivering and chattering in freezing houses, and eating abominable food.

More accurately, this book will tell you how to live like a Duke, a word pronounced in England with a yoop in it, or dee-yook, and not "dook", as you might say. Or, in fact, like our word "few". Repeat several times, "few Dukes", and you will have it. It is also a true statement. There are only thirty-two of them, and almost all of them do live in a manner to which you could become accustomed and which, with careful study of a few simple rules, you can easily attain.

2

How to Leave Home

LET US assume you have decided to cross the Atlantic, to improve the lot of people everywhere, including your own.

Be bold! This is not a mission for the timid, or the faint of heart.

However, there is no use being any bolder than necessary.

BE NEEDED

Though many do pay their fares abroad, this is not essential. It is better, and cheaper, to be needed abroad by someone. Anyone who needs you enough will be glad to pay all your expenses, and those of your whole family.

Find a company, preferably your own, which is sending people abroad. In these days of export drives, world leadership, and expansive thinking, people are being shipped and flown out by the thousand. Join them.

You will soon find there is no problem just being sent *anywhere*:

"Willing to travel, eh, Brash?"

"Oh, yes, sir, anywhere at all! Anxious to spread our way of life!"

(Always establish you are WILLING to go anywhere.)

"At the moment it needs spreading in the direction of Saudi Arabia."

"I'd certainly envy anyone going to a tropical paradise like that, sir!"

"You're the lucky boy, Brash."

"Just a matter of my framboesia, sir."

"Framboesia?"

"Yaws, sir. Lying dormant now. Just waiting till I get south of Suez."

"There's a nice cool spot in the Lapland branch."

"There we run head-on into my frostbite, sir. But I don't expect anything pleasant! I can stand up to the fog and rain and bone-chilling cold of England as well as the next man!"

Remember that the keynote is service and sacrifice. The man with selfish motives will not travel far.

BE BRITISH

You will find many little ways to show you are familiar with the British way of life. The black derby and tightly rolled umbrella will not be enough. Add a battered copy of the London *Financial Times*, and some well-chosen words:

"What do you favor today, sir? Ordin'ries or gilt edge?"

"Are you betting on the dogs again, Brash?"

"Forgot you don't follow the London market, sir. Pity, with this bank rate. License to steal."

Any bits and pieces of Old England will be valuable:

"What in hell are you doing with that canoe paddle, Brash?"

"Cricket bat, sir. Just trying to keep my eye in."

BE BILINGUAL

Let your leaders know, from the start, that there is a language problem, and you are on top of it. You will have to perform an occasional demonstration. This can be done without any real knowledge of the British language:

"Actually, what I said to him, sir, was——"

(Say twenty or thirty words in a British Public School accent. If you don't have one, just remember to keep your mouth almost closed, don't move your lips, never say the letter "r", and put a small eraser and a few paper clips in your mouth.)

"Dammit, Brash, I didn't understand a word you said!"

(Few Britons would, either, but no matter.)

"Oh, sorry, sir, thought you were bilingual. Let's chuck this British and go back to plain, honest American, shall we?"

Do other demonstrations when a rival is present:

"There! He did it again, Wilfing! Did you understand it?"

"Afraid not, sir."

"Just a trick, really, men. Few short months and you get almost every word."

You will make your point in no time:

"I was just thinking. That Brash lad. Not much to him, really, but he *does* understand the language."

FEATHER YOUR NEST

Bear in mind that you may be forgotten while you are abroad. If you don't feather your nest before leaving, you will find that your new location is far from the feathers.

Money alone need not be uppermost in your thoughts. You will be thinking of company prestige:

"A vice-president already, Brash—at your age?"

"In name only, sir. I understand the British are terribly sensitive to titles."

The money will be sure to follow.

ALLOW FOR THE COST OF LIVING

Establish at the outset that you will need an extra fixed percentage for the increased cost of living:

"What extra percentage does our company give for the added cost of living, sir?"

"*Extra*, Brash? It's a hell of a lot cheaper to live over there!"

"Just thinking of our Image, sir. Bringing the natives up to our standards, and all that."

BURN YOUR BOATS

The first year in England will be the hardest, especially for wives, who have to cope with the tricky little problems of living. It is wise to block any hasty or impulsive retreat.

Burn your boats:

"*Sell* our house, Buckley?"

"Never turn back! Faces forward!"

"What if we don't *like* it there?"

"Just picture this, Peg. You're in the rose garden at Brash Manor, having Lady Nyiff-Nyiff in for tiffin. The butler arrives, bows to you, and——"

"It *does* sound lovely, Buckley. Raise your feet, will you, so I can scrub under there, too?"

"The butler says, 'Madam, it's your tenant from the Colonies again, reversing the charges. He demands you do *something* about the cesspool.'"

"Perhaps we *should* sell, Buckley."

BON VOYAGE!

Soon all will be ready, and you will take off for a new life, and adventures undreamed of by your stay-at-home friends. Have courage! And pay close attention to the rules that follow.

3

Establish a Beach Head

YOU WILL find that Americans accumulate south and west of London, in the green countryside of Surrey, Middlesex, and Sussex. This is because the smog from London usually blows the other way.

Here you will find country houses galore, just waiting for you. In fact, you will find everyone is just waiting for you. Somehow they will all know you are still thinking in terms of a three-bedroom house on a blasted, bull-dozed sixth of an acre, for $65,000, and they will try to get you while the memory is still fresh.

Don't allow yourself to be rushed:

"Oh, Buckley you ought to *see* it! A whole acre of rhododendrons and roses, and a greenhouse, and—"

"House on it, too, Peg?"

Everyone is waiting for you.

17

"The *loveliest*, quaintest——"

"Did you get inside?"

"Well, not exactly——"

(They sometimes put this off, especially if there is a chill in the air.)

"But all for just $39,000, Buckley!"

"Smart girl!"

"Shall we sign the papers now?"

"Any day now, Peg. Wanted to tell you a story about a fellow in the office. Lovely old house. Whole roof collapsed. Some funny little beetles ate away all the rafters! Isn't that a riot?"

(You will find enough stories like this, all true, to hold off any abrupt action for months.)

It will take you at least a year to adopt a new sense of values. Meantime you will spend many happy hours rummaging around the British countryside.

Remember this simple rule: never buy a house until you have some close British friends look at it first with a jaundiced eye:

"Thirty-nine thousand dollars? That's fourteen thousand pounds, old boy! They saw you coming. Isn't worth a farthing over nine."

Meanwhile you will need shelter. Many Americans go through three stages: first, the country hotel, second, the rented flat or apartment, and third, a house of their own.

Your beach head, then, will be a hotel, preferably in the country, near the spot where you hope to settle.

Start digging in.

4

Hotels Can Be Fun

AFTER YOU have practiced your British by asking everyone about hotels, you can find one easily by looking in the yellow directory of the Automobile Association, which gives details and quotes prices.

Choose one in the middle of the area where you hope to find a home.

Your main purpose will be to rent a place quickly, especially if it is you, and not the company, who has to pay the bill. If you are paying, you will find that forty or fifty dollars a day for rooms and food helps remarkably to focus your mind.

GET TO KNOW YOUR CHILDREN

You may think you know your children well, but after several days in two hotel rooms with them, you will discover you scarcely knew them at all. You will get to know them much better. You may not *like* them better, but you will get to know them better.

"Honestly, Buckley, one more day of this and I am going to go stark, raving mad!"

"Just keep telling yourself they're on top of us because they like us, Peg."

"Why don't they act as though they *like* us?"

THINGS EVERYONE CAN DO

Soon you will all be living a busy, happy life, doing the many things everyone can do in a hotel. No matter where you and the children look you will find something fascinating.

You'll find all kinds of people coming to your rooms.

1. Bells are everywhere

No need to tell the children about the bells. Before long they will discover them for themselves. After that you will find all kinds of people coming up to your rooms, at all hours. If you give them all money they will go away. Luckily, a sixpence, worth seven cents, brings larger smiles in a British hotel than a quarter does in the U.S.A.

2. Fun in the elevators

The lifts will be a source of endless amusement for the children, who will spend happy hours riding up and down.

"My goodness, your cute little elevator is stuck between the second and third floor, with our children in it!"

"*All* your children, Madam?"

"All but the little one. He's riding in the laundry hamper."

"They'll be quite safe, Madam. We'll do our best to get them down before nightfall."

(*You will find that some things in England take the longest time.*)

3. Keys and how to use them

The British have discovered locks on doors, and keys. Your children will be close behind them.

"I want to lock the door, Mommy!"

"No, *I* want to!"

"It's *my* turn to!"

Soon all the keys to all the doors will be lost.

"We just wondered if the chamber maid had a pass key we could use to get in."

"Madam, the chamber maid is missing, too. We have reason to believe she is locked in the linen room."

4. The wonder world of electricity

While the children are playing with the hotel, you can have fun, too. Gone are the hum–drum days of American electricity, just plugging things in. A simple thing like trying to use a travel iron can be an adventure:

"Buckley, I *know* they have 240 volts. I just flip the switch to here, where it says 240."

"Then you're all set."

"Only one thing. There isn't any outlet."

"I found that out when I tried to shave."

But the traveller, far from home, must never say die.

"It took me an hour, Buckley, but I did find an outlet. It's camouflaged behind the wardrobe in the children's room. When you're out today, get an extension cord, will you?"

(You will discover that the adventure has only begun.)

"Oh, you mean a flex, sir."

"I guess so, yes, a wire like that. But with a plug in the end."

"Yes, sir. Three-pin five amp? Two-pin fifteen amp? Three-pin power plug?"

"Just a plug. So I can plug it into the wall."

"We have seventeen different kinds of plugs, sir."

"Why?"

"No one knows why, sir."

You will find it is best to take a wax impression, and bring it to the electrician. In no time you will be able to plug in the iron.

"Oh, Buckley! All the lights went out!"

"Must have blown a fuse. I'll phone and get them to screw in a new one."

(Hours will go by. Sometimes days.)

"Still no lights, Peg?"

"I had a long talk with the manager this morning, Buckley. He's very nice and he's doing everything he can. They've already found seven fuse boxes, but it isn't in any of them."

"No!"

"You have to remember the hotel was made out of five houses, each one with three or four fuse boxes and at least two different electrical circuits. He says that—"

Before you know it, the lights will be on again. You

will be advised, however, not to plug the iron into the room outlet. There will be another room, two floors down, in the laundry, with a different circuit. And, of course, a different plug.

5. Try the Telly

The British satisfy the normal, healthy blood-lust of children the same way Americans do, and with the same programs. Once in front of the TV, the children will feel right at home:

"Buckley, there's a little disagreement in the television room. It was a choice between some political program and cowboys, and our group tipped the majority to cowboys. Feeling is running pretty high."

"Not to worry, Peg." *(Get used to new expressions.)* "We're getting a telly of our own tomorrow."

"Not *buying* one!"

(At this stage you may hesitate to make any permanent investments in Britain. It will be a passing phase.)

"Nobody buys tellies here, they all rent them. Just a few pounds down, and ten and six a week."

(Translation: ten shillings and sixpence, or $1.47.)

Unlike America, where television never stops, day or night, in England the telly is on very little in the morning, and only spasmodically in the afternoon.

Whether you like it or not, you'll have to make expeditions to places like the Tower of London, Madame Tussaud's, and Battersea Park.

For these jaunts, and for the main business of finding a house or apartment, you will need to do a lot of driving. Be sure to study the next chapter carefully.

5

How to Drive a MOW-tah-cah

IN BRITAIN there are no automobiles, but millions of MOW-tah-cahs.

You will never again in your life be so dangerous to your fellow man as in your first few hours of driving a motor-car. A maniac running amuck with a shotgun could not be a greater menace.

Let us assume you have a valid American driving license. You are free to hire a car immediately, and drive it among the natives. Not only will you be hurled, untutored, into the most dangerous traffic in the world, but you will be expected to drive on the wrong side of the road, will be sitting behind a steering wheel on the right-hand side of the car, shifting gears for perhaps the first time in years, and with the wrong hand.

"Something wrong with this gear lever, Peg."

"Buckley, you're shifting the direction signals. The gear is on the other side."

(Your next thought, of sheer horror, is that they have reversed the clutch and brake pedals, too—but they have not.)

You will not be required to carry DANGER signs or other warning devices, and will not be preceded by motorcycle policemen or others to warn the populace against you. You will be driving on the narrowest, twistiest roads you have ever seen, scarcely wide enough for two cars to pass without touching, and with a layer of moving bicycles on each side.

"Oh, Buckley, I can't look!"

"Well, I *have* to, Peg."

"You ran that bicycle into the ditch, Daddy!"

"Yay!"

"Buckley, you missed that car by *one* inch."

"Shall we walk?"

You will soon see why the British win most of the driving championships. It is the law of the survival of the fittest. If you are not an expert driver in England you will soon be dead.

It will not be (as we shall see later) until you have driven for many months—if you survive—and have become as experienced and as safe as anyone can be, that the hand of traffic officialdom will descend sternly upon you.

TAKE YOUR TIME

The British roads were built by the Romans. They have deteriorated to some extent in all that time.

At first you will worry that you are not on the "main road" or "highway", and will ask directions:

"Oh, uh, Mac——"

"I beg your pardon?"

"I mean, pardon me, sir, can you tell me how to get to the main road to London?"

"The *main* road?"

"The highway, the turnpike, the—to *London*, you know."

"London? Straight on!"

There are almost no "main roads" as you know them. The only road between two major cities may be two cars wide, a winding lane with no over or under passes, going through the center of every village, with all its stop lights, shopping carts, bicycles, children, and dogs. There are only about two hundred miles of "thru-ways" (called Motorways) in the whole United Kingdom.

As a rule of thumb you can estimate a sixty mile an hour average in inter-city touring in America, Germany, or parts of Italy; about forty-five to fifty in France, and about twenty-five in England.

"Oh, Buckley, isn't it *lovely*!"

"Sure, is, pet."

"Daddy! Watch out!"

In England, when touring is inevitable, relax and enjoy it.

SOME RULES FOR BRITISH DRIVING

Later you will have to learn some wondrous rules to pass your British Driving Test. First, however, you must learn how to convert from American to British driving, and stay alive.

Just follow these simple rules:

1. Watch your left

You may be terrified by driving on the left, but you won't forget to do it. There is nothing like a solid line of traffic coming at you on your right to remind you. You will have trouble in three ways:

(*a*) *Reversing.* If you discover, on a lonely road, that you are going the wrong way, turn into a driveway and reverse, the chances are that you will go back on the right hand side. No one knows why this is true, but it is.

(*b*) *Right hand, left hand.* Because the right hand turn is the cross-traffic, or difficult turn, you will often confuse right turns with left turns.

"He said to turn *left*, Buckley."

"I did."

"No, you turned right."

"Daddy, don't you know your left hand?"

Don't use the words "right" and "left". Point, and say "this way!"

(*c*) *Watch your curbs*. The most dangerous thing about left hand driving is not when you are driving, but when you are walking across the street. You will look gaily to your left, step off the curb ("kerb" in British) and be missed by six inches—if you're lucky—by a car coming from your right.

2. Forget the lane: aim at the hole

You have been taught to drive in lanes, keeping parallel to the center of the road. Forget this quickly. Driving in Britain is never parallel to anything. You will be like a snake on a zig-zag obstacle course. Aim at the hole, up ahead, between the lorry and the two bicycles.

BEWARE OF ROUNDABOUTS

One theory of traffic is to speed it along and make it flow. The other is the British theory, to slow it down and harry it with obstacles, like fences in a steeplechase. The best example of this is the roundabout, a small, tight traffic circle. Whenever two British roads intersect there is a roundabout.

Once they tried to make rules to regulate the traffic whirling about in roundabouts and establish a right of way. After months of experimentation it was decided: it is not possible. Now the rule is: every man for himself.

Whenever foreign traffic experts are brought to Britain, they take one look at the roundabouts and flee in terror. "A traffic circle," said one, "is all right except when there is any real traffic. Then it leads to chaos."

Every time you get up enough speed to shift into high, you will come to a roundabout, a maelstrom of cars, whirling in circles, with no right of way. Your only weapon is bluff and bravado.

But remember, out of Britain's roundabouts have come the finest Grand Prix drivers in the world.

HOW TO PARK

In American cities it is easy to tell where you cannot park. It is always clearly marked. The answer usually is that you cannot park anywhere. The signs say, NO PARKING. In New York they even put up paper signs, on special occasions, such as parades, saying NO PARKING TODAY on top of the permanent sign saying NO PARKING ANY TIME.

In England you will find the problem is different. Many streets are not marked at all. You will think this means you can park. But you are suspicious. You find a policeman:

"Pardon me, constable——"

(You may call him "officer", too, the way you do at home.)

"Yes, sir?"

(They are the politest and most helpful policemen in the world.)

"Could you tell me if I can park here?"

"No, sir."

"You mean it's against the law to park here?"

"No, sir."

"Then it's all right to park here?"

"I didn't say that, sir."

"Would you give me a ticket if I did?"

"No, sir."

You park, and find your car has been towed away. The police at the towaway lot will be polite, will charge you a small fine, and let you have your car.

"Why did you tow it away?"

"It was causing an obstruction, sir."

"But it wasn't in front of a driveway, or anything— and I *asked a policeman*!"

"Did he give you permission to park?"

"He didn't say I *couldn't* park."

There is nothing illegal
about this at all.

"He couldn't give you *permission*. That would be illegal. If any of the Queen's subjects wishes to use a portion of any road, it is illegal to obstruct it. It is illegal even to stand still on the pavement *(translation: sidewalk)* if someone wishes to go by."

You can never be entirely sure. When in doubt, use parking meters, which are springing up everywhere. No good pointing out that by the above definition they are all completely illegal.

DO NOT BE AFRAID OF BICYCLES

All Americans, at first, are terrified of bicycles. You will be, too. It is like elephants and mice. You will think all

bicycle riders are twelve years old. In England some of them are fifty-two years old, wearing bowler hats, or sun-bonnets, but it won't make you feel any better. You will still try to give them three feet of clearance, and this will bring you almost over to the bicycles on the *other* side, to say nothing of the cars. You will even find bicycles riding abreast at five miles an hour, blocking the whole road. There is nothing illegal about this at all.

Pretty soon you will be so nervous you will be shaking. If you are a woman you will cry. Then you will get over it and drive like the British, just as though the bicycles were not there. In fact, fewer of them are there all the time, not only because of that, but because of affluence, and mini-cars.

"SHOULD I BE FRIGHTENED OF JAGUARS?"

Many English believe that all Jaguar drivers are predatory, vicious, and dangerous. After you buy *your* Jaguar (as most Americans do—here they cost much less than a Chevrolet) you will realize that this may be true of *other* Jaguar drivers, but it is not true of you.

"Z" IS FOR ZEBRA

A zebra (pronounced ZEB-ra, not ZEE-bra) crossing is for pedestrians. It is a black and white strip across a road, with flashing yellow lights at the side. If a pedestrian even puts his foot on a zebra the law says that all traffic must stop until he is across.

You might think that in places where there are crowds of pedestrians it would stop traffic completely. This is right. It does.

There are also a few "panda" crossings, with triangular black and white areas, and a stop light that the pedestrian can push.

WATCH YOUR LANGUAGE

Almost all words connected with cars and driving are different in British. Here are a few, the American word first, followed by the British translation: windshield/ windscreen; fender/wing; parking lights/side lights; trunk/boot; tire/tyre; hood/bonnet; convertible top/ hood; generator/dynamo; wrench/spanner; crank/ starting handle; pass/overtake; overpass/flyover; shoulder/verge; roadside parking space/layby; divided roadway/dual carriageway; turnpike, parkway, or freeway/motorway; truck/lorry; underpass/subway; subway/underground; sedan/saloon; convertible/ drophead; gasoline/petrol; trailer/caravan; trailer truck/articulated lorry; panel truck/van.

Finally, remember that the American word "impossible" and the British word "impassable" are pronounced exactly the same way:

"Pardon me, sir. How's the road?"

"Impassable."

"Well, I guess they're *all* impossible—but is it passable?"

You will think by now that your driving adventures will all be over, but this will not be so.

The worst, indeed, is yet to come—but there is no time now to wait for *that*.

6

How to Choose an Apartment

IF YOU have survived the British roads, you will be ready
to rent an apartment, or perhaps even a house.

FIND A REAL-ESTATE AGENT

It is easy to find a real-estate agent as soon as you stop
looking in the "r's". Look up "Estate Agents". The
British do not know what the word "real" in front of
"estate" means. Americans do not know, either, but they
use it just the same.

In America there are more than enough real-estate
agents for everyone. In England they do not have enough
to go around. This is why an American agent feels you
are doing him a favor to ride in his car with him, and be
taken from house to house.

In Britain, the estate agent is doing *you* a favor. He
will make an appointment to see you, at a time that is
convenient to him, at his office, and will tell you what is
for rent. He will be so pleasant and charming you will
wish you could take him with you to the house, but you
cannot. He will have to stay there, and he has another
appointment with somebody else in half an hour.
Getting to the places will be up to you.

While you are talking to him, do not forget to ask
about the heating, even if it is summer. Winter is sure
to come.

HOW TO ASK ABOUT CENTRAL HEATING

If you come from any northern state, you will find that your first winter in England is the mildest you have ever spent—*outdoors*, and by far the coldest you have ever spent—*indoors*.

People will tell you about the British attitude toward heating houses, but you will not believe it. No one ever believes it until the first winter is over. The British are the only people in the civilized world who still refuse to heat their houses when it's cold outside.

In England it is cold enough to suffer, but not quite cold enough to die. The British do not mind suffering, with the cold, or with anything else. They believe there is a moral advantage to it, and that it is immoral to be comfortable.

The more you criticize them about this the more defensive they become. They now attribute all human ills to central heating. It will give you colds, crack your membranes, ruin your furniture, wreck your house, and destroy your moral fiber.

Therefore, you must be careful how you broach the subject of central heating to the real estate man:

"Uh, can you tell me about the *heating*?"

"Oh, yes, Mr. Brash! You Americans!"

(He will laugh indulgently.)

"I mean, does it have central heating?"

"Yes, of course, Mr. Brash! Regular American-style central heating! Radiators and all!"

"Oh, fine."

You will have a feeling of warmth, and security, until you discover that the words "central heating" and "radiators" are meaningless, like the words "custom

35

made" in American advertisements. They are status words.

"Central heating" in Britain usually refers to one or two radiators in a hallway or in the living room. They are sometimes fed from the hot water system. Sometimes there is a hot water coil in the coal stove in the kitchen which heats a radiator or two. This is for "background heating", which means it will prevent water from freezing in the wash bowls. Temperatures away from open fires will still be about fifty degrees.

Ask how many radiators there are, what kind of a furnace heats them, and try to find out what the winter temperature will be without using open fires, or kerosene (called "paraffin"), gas, or electric heaters. Most British homes use all these methods, plus bed warmers, and hot water bottles in a growing panic as the temperature drops toward freezing point.

There is growing panic as the temperature drops.

BUY AN ATLAS

If you are looking in London, or its outskirts, buy an atlas, or street guide. Get the one in color which costs a dollar. You will not be able to find anything without it.

There are no grid plans or numbered streets. If you are in the country, get a good map. Even with them you will be lost, most of the time.

MODERN IS FOR THE LOWER CLASSES

On your way, maps in hand, hunting for the first address, you will pass some of the most modern apartment houses you have ever seen.

You will then arrive at your address, which will probably be a flat carved out of a remodelled Victorian house. Chances are you will be disappointed, and you will telephone your estate agent:

"Well, we did see the apartment, I mean the flat, in the old house."

"Good, Mr. Brash. Will you take it?"

"We were hoping we could find something a bit more modern. Now just three or four blocks away—"

"I beg your pardon?"

(The word "block" has no meaning in British, except as in "block of flats", or apartment building.)

"I mean a quarter of a mile away—those five big new twelve story buildings. Very modern, you know?"

"Well, those really aren't for *your* kind of people, Mr. Brash!"

"We *are* prepared to pay just a *little* more. How much are they?"

"About two pounds a week."

"Hey, Peg, he says those terrific modern apartments are less than six bucks a week!"

"Take one now, Buckley!"

"We'll take one!"

"You couldn't do that, Mr. Brash. Those are

council flats, for low income families—and there's a waiting list of thousands."

In America, modern is for the rich; in Britain it is for the lower classes.

This is because in Britain everybody wants to be like the Upper Classes, who live in very old houses. People with new money try to buy the old houses, but there are not enough to go around, so they buy land and build old houses. You may think it is hard to build an old house, but they do it just the same. They are building new Victorian houses all over England. They never really look as good as new, but after they weather for a few years they look as good as old.

The modern architects had to go to agencies like the London County Council to build apartments for low-income people. Some of them are the most modern buildings in Europe, and the poor people have to live in them whether they want to or not.

So it is now firmly established that modern is for the working classes. Nobody else would touch it with a ten foot pole.

YES, THERE *IS* A PLACE FOR AMERICANS

Do not worry. They are saving a place for you. There are certain places reserved just for Americans. They do not show them to anyone else. Down through the years Americans have always rented them, ever since the last war, and in some cases even the war before *that*.

The place that is waiting for you has been rented by all kinds of Americans, who have had only one thing in common: they didn't renew the lease. If you knew this at first you would wonder why not. But not for very long.

Some of these places will be whole houses, and some will be parts of very large houses, cut up into flats. They will be different in many ways, but they will have most, if not all, of the following characteristics:

1. You have been here before

Something about it is just what you expected to find in England, couldn't get at home, and are sure is a voice out of your past saying: "You have been here before." It convinces you this is just the way your ancestors must have lived, all evidence to the contrary. It may be a dining room that looks like a gothic cathedral, a living room panelled in dark oak, a thatched roof, or a collection of Elizabethan beams. The ancestors of other Americans may have been farmers, weavers, debtors, or horse thieves, but yours lived here, and the way you feel standing here proves it.

Whatever the nature of the wonder-thing is, it must be powerful enough to make you overlook the kitchen, or make you sign the lease before you see it.

The estate agent is a sensitive man. He feels, too, that you have been here before, and he felt that with the other Americans when he rented it to them. They had been here before, too.

In fact, he is so sensitive that his price may vary somewhat according to how much you were here before, and how deeply you feel about it.

Therefore, keep your head, and mask your true feelings. Be polite, but not too impressed. Here are a few good phrases:

"Well, what did you think of it, Mr. Brash?"

"Ah, about that panelling in the living room."

"I know. All Americans fall in love with that, Mr. Brash." (The British are more likely to be concerned that it is crawling with woodworm.)

"It is nice in a way, but a bit dark. You suppose they'd mind if we hid it with wall-length drapes?"

Or, in the case of thatched roofs, which are to Americans like catnip to cats:

"About that thatched roof—"

"Bit of Old England, isn't it, Mr. Brash?"

"Bit too old, I'm afraid."

"*All* the Americans are so enthusiastic about it—"

"The *new* Americans, you mean. Hate the drip, drip, drip after every shower, myself. Any chance of a proper roof being put in?"

You will think of others yourself.

2. A garden

The garden will almost *always* be the most beautiful you have ever seen. We shall take up this whole massive subject in a later chapter. At the moment, your best approach is:

"Well, yes, it *is* an interesting little garden."

"After all, Mr. Brash, it's what you're really paying for."

"Gardener's included in the price, of course?"

(He will not be, but you will have scored a point.)

3. It will be furnished,

whether you want it to be or not. This will make possible a rental price that would turn an Englishman pale.

The furniture in most of these houses was originally

either (*a*) antique, or (*b*) old. The antiques were sold at auction long ago, to other Americans. What will be left will be heavy Victorian pieces in an advanced state of dilapidation.

"Do you think they'd mind if we just stored the furniture?"

"Oh, no, Mr. Brash. Most of the Americans do store it."

"And then pay the unfurnished rate?"

"Oh, no, sir!"

"Just for kicks, what is the unfurnished rate?"

"I don't even know that, sir."

(You will discover later it is half, or a third what you are paying.)

4. It will have the appearance of central heating

For example, it may have an impressive number of radiators, and a large furnace. Everyone knows that Americans almost always move during the summer, when central heating is never on, no matter how cold it is.

"But is it really warm in winter?"

"Ask anyone, Mr. Brash. They say this is the warmest house for miles around."

(This may be true, but the moment of real truth will not come until later.)

HOW TO FIND YOUR KITCHEN

Your have signed the lease and the place is yours. Let us say your new home is the ground floor of an enormous Manor House, which originally had twenty bedrooms, and is now divided into flats, of which yours is the largest.

Your "reception rooms" (i.e., all rooms where you "receive" people, such as the living room or lounge, dining room, drawing room, library, or whatever, as opposed to bedrooms, etc.) will be enormous, panelled and vaulted. Some of them will have been converted into bedrooms, because the original bedrooms, all upstairs, are outside your flat.

It will be weeks before you discover the wonders that lie in every nook and cranny.

If the magic of old England has done its work, you haven't thought of the workaday things like kitchens. You may even have assumed that, like everything else, it would be too fabulous to believe. This is not always the case:

"You suppose there is a kitchen, Peg?"

"*Must* be, Buckley."

"It's not anywhere around here. What's all that around *there*?"

"The billiard room."

"No table."

"I thought we'd make it into a sort of nursery-gymnasium."

"There's a long corridor going east, this way. Like to try it?"

"We might drop pieces of paper, Buckley, to find our way back."

"What are all *these* little rooms?"

"Maids' rooms, he said. Used to be six maids."

"And this one?"

"It was a servant's sitting room. Might use it for TV."

"What's up ahead there, Peg, the dungeon?"

"I don't know. It's too dark to see."

"Must be a light around somewhere."

KITCHENS ARE FOR SCULLERY MAIDS

Before you face the kitchen, remember that the lady who built the house never intended to enter it. The kitchen was for slaves. There was a cook and a scullery maid, and another maid whose job was to get the food all that way into the dining room. The window, if any, looks out onto the bare brick wall of the back of the stables, or the potting shed. There are bars on the windows. (Opinion is divided as to whether they were to keep the scullery maids in, or the peasants out.)

"Oh, my, Buckley, I feel so—so enclosed—like in a submarine!"

"Cheer up, Peg, look at those appliances! New refrigerator, deep freeze, dishwasher, electric stove, washing machine, dryer!"

"They *are* lovely—and all American, too!"

Often you will discover that the previous tenants have brought elaborate equipment from America, especially if they were sent by the armed forces, or large companies. This material cannot, however, be legally sold without payment of import duties and purchase taxes that total more than the cost of the items themselves.

Do not be surprised if the equipment is removed.

"Oh, Buckley, have you seen the kitchen? They took all the American things out!"

"Spoke to George about that. They have to move everything. He says they've spent sixty dollars of the company's money just moving around a garbage can. He told 'em he could buy a new one for three bucks, but they can't put that on the books."

"But there isn't anything left but a wooden sink, a coal stove, and an old table!"

Though the kitchen may be bare, do not worry that your wife will be lonesome in it. You will all be there with her. The first two or three meals you will try to carry the food into the dining room, a quarter of a mile away. After that you will all eat in the kitchen. It will become the Family Room.

GETTING SETTLED IN YOUR NEW HOME

Before you know it you will feel you have lived here always. The long weeks before your trunks and boxes come will pass quickly.

"Buckley, how can we eat? No plates, no knives or forks, not even a lamp to see by!"

"No problem, Peg. Agent gave me a key to the box room. Everything we need's in there, he says."

Every English house has a box room, or storage area of some kind. In it you will discover the debris of Empire, and the relics of a by-gone way of life.

"Buckley, all I wanted were some plates and forks and glasses—and look! Five boar spears, a roll of garden party tickets, three croquet mallets with warped handles, a solar topee, five Chinese lacquer bowls, and this four foot bronze statue of Mercury, holding a light bulb."

"Put him on the table. We'll light him up and eat dinner in the Chinese bowls."

"It'll have to be cold. I still can't figure out how to light the coal stove."

THE LANDLORD IS YOUR FRIEND

Though you will seldom see your landlord, he will be your friend and protector. He will consider that you are, like all colonial peoples, a burden he has to bear, for a price.

However, it is well to remember that the renting laws were all written by landlords, and for landlords. The careless American may find himself saying: "I think these rooms need to be painted." The landlord will always agree, as long as you're talking about the *inside*. In England the landlord pays only for the *outside*. The inside is up to you.

You will discover the debris of Empire.

7

Now, Off to School!

ONCE YOU have got the stove going, you will begin to think about sending the children off to school. You will probably go about it in a simple, child-like American manner:

"Oh, pardon me, can you tell me where the school bus stops?"

"The—ah—school—*bus?*"

(You will wonder if you have used the wrong word again, but you have not. The British word for "bus" is "bus", also.)

"Well, I mean—where do the children go to school?"

"Well—*everywhere*, really!"

(This is true. In England schools are everywhere, and that is where your children will go, in all directions.)

"I saw a beautiful building a few streets down. Is *that* a school? It looks like one."

"Oh, *that.* That's a *council* school."

(This will be said in a strange tone which you will not at first understand.)

BEWARE OF MODERN SCHOOLS

You will soon discover that "council" or "state" schools are what you think of as "public" schools. They are free. Everyone knows that in England "Public Schools" are *not* free. It is a kind of British doublespeak. Public Schools are the most private, and the most expensive, of all.

The most important thing for you to remember about British schools is that free schooling is not considered really respectable. People like you, who send your children to free schools in the States (at least until they get to the university) never send them to free schools in England. It is a social error.

You do not need to worry that you won't be able to tell the schools apart. You can tell by the outside of the buildings, and it is the same as it is with apartment houses. Modern is for the lower classes. Beautiful, glass-walled modern buildings are for the children of unskilled

The more ancient the building, the more they will learn.

workers, and are free. Medieval ruins are for the children of managing directors, and peers of the realm.

The more ancient the building, the higher will be the fees, the shorter the term, the more likely the children are to be beaten with sticks and (many say) the more they will learn.

"Should we," so many Americans ask, "send our children to the modern schools?" Perhaps we should start at the beginning.

ASK YOUR NEIGHBORS

Every time you go out to have a drink with either your British friends, your resident-American friends, or both of them together, topic A (and B, and C) will be schools. Even if you have no children of school age, you will have to know about this, if only for conversation.

Let us say your wife is questioning a neighbor, an English woman who may well be the nicest neighbor you have ever had, as soon as you get used to her funny way of talking:

"Oh, dear, Mrs. Price-Johnson, you must feel very lucky not to have children!"

"Goodness, we have two!"

"Oh? I've never seen them."

"They're away at boarding school."

(All children from professional class homes go away to boarding school. During school terms middle-class suburbs are completely childless. You may think this would be expensive. It is. It costs more than a thousand dollars a year for each child. For many professional Britons about half their income after taxes goes for school fees.)

"Well, I was just looking for a good grade school, and a junior high, and a high-school."

"I beg your pardon?"

(You will discover there are no "grade schools", or even "grades" as you know them, or "junior high schools" or "high schools".)

"I mean, just the local free schools. Couldn't I get the children in?"

"Yes, they'd take them. Of course there are about fifty in each class."

"How many in the classes at the boarding schools?"

"Fifteen, twenty. The teachers are paid more, too."

"Well, why don't the P.-T.A.'s *do* something about it?"

"The *whats*?"

(There are no Parent-Teacher Associations, in the American sense, though there are parent associations, which come to listen to Christmas carols or speech days. They have no real power to change the school.)

"If you don't have P.-T.A.'s—who *runs* the schools?"

"The headmasters."

(This is always a profound shock to Americans.)

"What about that little school down the street, in the old house. Is *that* a free school?"

"No, it's private. It's a cram school for the eleven-plus."

"What's the eleven-plus?"

"All children take it at eleven. If they pass they can go to a grammar school."

(Grammar schools are virtually the only free schools that take children up to university level. They are day schools, something like American Prep Schools. Some

grammar schools used to be private schools before the war. Their academic standards are high. But only about one child in five passes the eleven-plus.)

"What happens if they fail the eleven-plus?"

"If they can't afford private schools they have to go to secondary-modern schools."

(There are a few "comprehensive" schools, something like American junior high and high schools, but almost all the four out of five children who fail the eleven-plus go to secondary modern schools, which seem to Americans like vocational schools, and sometimes even like schools for backward children. Some have an atmosphere of abandon-hope-all-ye-who-enter-here. Most of the students leave them at fifteen or sixteen to go to work.)

"If your children passed the eleven-plus, Mrs. Price-Johnson, would you send them to a grammar school?"

"One of mine did pass, but I didn't send him. We feel the boarding schools are better for their characters."

CHARACTER IS WHAT YOU ARE BUYING

The British, like you, are interested in character. It is noteworthy, also, that almost every position at the top in Britain is held by a Public (i.e., Private Boarding) School man.

Some say this is because of their characters, and some say it is because of the ties they wear, the "old school ties" you have heard about. The ties do not give them character; they show that it is there.

It is as difficult for a "grammar school boy" to get to the top in England as it is for a high school graduate who

The ties do not *give* them character, they show that it is there.

didn't go to a university to get ahead in America: very difficult, but not entirely impossible.

It is also worth noting that a high percentage of former grammar school men who succeed do not send their sons back to grammar schools, but send them to Public Schools.

Most Englishmen, even in the upper classes, get all the character they need by the time they are 17 or 18, and rarely go to a university at all. Only one Briton in 25 does go, compared with 1 in 3 in America.

Be careful when you ask an Englishman: "Where did you go to school?" which, in American terms means, "Where did you go to high school?" It is a sensitive question, like asking how much money he makes, or whether he has any hereditary diseases.

HOW TO FIND A PRIVATE SCHOOL

You will resist, almost to the death, sending your children to boarding school. All Americans do, at first. It seems to you inhuman, un–American, and a violation of the doctrine of together-ness.

This will make things more difficult, but you will find a few private day schools scattered widely around the countryside.

The first dozen or so that you talk to will be completely full. All English schools are completely full. Children are entered at birth. (It should be added here that even if you are willing to send them to a boarding school, a vacancy is even harder to find, though you can range farther afield.)

However, after months of effort, and with the help of all your British friends, you will locate several schools. It is an unwritten rule that each of your children, no matter how many you have, will go to a different school, each at least five miles from your house, each in a different direction, and none with a school bus.

There are several reasons for this: one is that the British believe no good will come of mixing the sexes; almost all schools are mono–sexual. Another reason is that all schooling is compartmented elaborately by age: some go only to eleven, some to thirteen, others from thirteen to seventeen, and so on. A third reason is that schools rarely have more than one free place, anyway.

Each school will be very difficult to locate:

"This is the address, Buckley, but I don't see any school."

"What's *that*?"

"An old house, like ours. Probably cut up into flats."

"See that wooden sign under the bush?
'BLANDFIELD SCHOOL.'"

All the schools will be like this, in Victorian houses. Once you have found them, all your troubles will be over. You will only have to dress the children and work out some way to get them there every day.

PLIMSOLLS ARE NOT WATER WINGS

All British school children wear uniforms, usually grey with colored "blazers" or jackets. Boys up to about thirteen wear shorts, even in the dead of winter. You would think their knees would turn blue, and this is right. They do.

They will give you a list, about a foot long, with every item on it. A few words will need explaining. You will see on each list: "one pair of plimsolls". These are not water wings, as many American mothers think, but canvas and rubber shoes, usually black, like sneakers. British children change from their outdoor shoes to plimsolls whenever they come inside. They even carry them to parties, and leave their muddy shoes outside—another proof that British civilization is ahead of America in many ways.

You will be sure they made a mistake about "knickers", which they have put on the girls' list, and not the boys'. It is not a mistake. Knickers are for school girls. They are like what grandma called "bloomers", and are worn under skirts.

The other funny word, which usually goes right along with knickers, is "liners". These are underpants, worn under the knickers. Knickers and liners. Say them together several times and you'll remember.

Every item you can put a needle into must have a name tape sewed on it, like the tapes you sewed on when they went to camp, only more so. There will be at least a hundred for each child. You will spend many happy hours by the fireside.

Finally they will all be ready, and assembled in uniform. The boys will look somewhat more orderly, and generally improved. The girls will look like inmates of a good Victorian orphanage. You may think you will never get used to seeing them like this, but you will. You will soon forget they looked any other way.

ASSEMBLE YOUR EQUIPMENT

Getting them all to school every day will take planning. It will be like organizing an amphibious landing. Long before D-Day you will have to accumulate and count-down a list of equipment:

1. Protective clothing

Remember that the children will spend hours in the open air. This may mean rain! Uniforms usually include warm raincoats. You will want to add waterproof duffle coats with hood, for boys, and rubber boots (called "Wellingtons") for both sexes.

2. Bicycles

All children must have efficient bicycles, equipped with working lamps, white in front, and red in rear. In England it gets dark about 4 p.m. in winter, and they will often be cycling home in the pitch dark.

Get a puncture repair kit and practice removing

wheel and inner tube and repairing puncture. The first time you do this it will take all day. When you can do it in ten minutes, you are ready.

3. Station wagon,

called "estate car". Before buying, make sure the cargo deck is large enough to hold a bike. Most British station wagons will. You will often need it for emergency rescue operations, miles from home.

4. Knapsacks, duffle bags

Few British schools seem to be equipped with anything resembling lockers, or places to keep things. Your children will move tons of equipment, carrying books, notebooks, soccer boots, lacrosse sticks, cricket bats, and so on, back and forth every day. Make sure each container can be tied or strapped either to the child, or to the bicycle.

D-DAY AT LAST

Actually, there is no one D-Day, since all private schools open and close on different days, but it is wise to have the whole operation planned:

"You all set, Peg?"

"I think so, Buckley. Susan goes by bike two miles to the station, gets the train, and then walks a mile to school. Pete does his whole three miles by bike——"

"What about my cello, Mom?"

"On cello days I'll have to take you——"

"Then what about *me*, Mom?"

"For you, Ted, I think I've got Mrs Evans to sort of car-pool with me, and on cello days——"

"Dad, my bike has a flat."

"And mine goes flap-flap-ickle every time the wheel goes around——"

"Boy, oh boy, Peg, we'll sure look forward to week-ends!"

WEEKENDS ARE FOR RELAXING

You will be able to sleep a little later on week-ends.

"Hey, Dad, I don't have anybody to play with."

"Me, neither, Dad."

"Play with each other!"

"He won't play with *me*, I'm too little!"

"Aren't there any kids in the neighborhood?"

(There will not be. They will all be at boarding school. Your children's friends will be from their day schools.)

"Nigel wants me to come over, Mom."

"Who brings who?"

"His mother doesn't have the car now."

"If they ride their bikes to school, Peg, can't they ride over?"

"Nigel's on the other side of school. It's six miles each way, and pouring rain."

"If you take *him*, Mom, you've got to take me to Crispin's."

'Your mother doesn't *got* to do anything!"

"Now, Buckley!"

You will have many opportunities, every weekend, to drive miles and miles through the lovely English countryside.

STAND FIRM

Stand firm, and you will show your British friends that the boarding school is not necessary, and that it is possible to have together-ness, in all directions at once.

It is only after you get older, and physical exhaustion begins to set in, that you may yield to a less vigorous way of life:

"Dad, how come Pete gets to go to boarding school and not me?"

"Well, right now that's how the cookie crumbles."

"What's a cookie, Dad?"

(Already America is beginning to recede.)

"It's sort of like a sweet biscuit, mate."

And if you keep your eyes open, you will notice many things:

"Peg! Did you see the list of subjects Pete is taking this year? English composition, English literature, history, geography, French, Latin, pure mathematics, physics, chemistry, biology, and music!"

"You left out scripture."

"Wow! At thirteen!"

There will be times when you will think it is all worth while.

8

"Do I WANT My Daughter to be a Duchess?"

Part I

IF YOU have a daughter approaching romantic age, leave her at home, with friends. Do not bring her to England.

It will seem to you, at first, that England is not a dangerous place for growing girls. It may even seem to you that it is far safer than America:

"Oh, Buckley, I'm so glad we have Susan in England, at this age."

(You will have just seen her in her orphan-asylum outfit, the man's tie, the flat heels, the man's sport jacket, and the Victorian hat.)

"She *does* look pretty repulsive, doesn't she, Peg?"

"When I think of the teen-age girls at home at this age—make-up plastered on an inch thick, convertibles, juke boxes, late dances—well, Susan just seems so *safe*!"

Impoverished lords and their mothers are waiting
behind every hedgerow.

THE DANGER IS ALL AROUND

She will not be quite as safe as you think, and the danger will not always lie within *her*:

"Just think, Buckley, last night Susan was dancing with the son of Lady Fitzwilliams!"

"Gosh, Peg, he's a Lord? The kid?"

"Actually, Father, Philip is just an 'Honourable', and his father is only a sort of Irish baronet———"

"Just think, Buckley! Lady Susan!"

"Oh, Mother, please! Actually Philip's father sells Jaguars, and they live in quite a small place, really!"

Perils will be everywhere. You may not be tempted by an Irish baronet, but where will you stop? Do you really want your daughter to be a Duchess? If you do, she will never be truly safe as long as there is an unmarried Duke in England.

Impoverished lords and their mothers are waiting behind every hedgerow, all too ready to trap American girls, and trade musty titles for hard American cash.

This is a problem that will never leave you, and one that we shall have to return to, again and again.

9

How to Dress in England

MEANWHILE, life will go on, and you will have to dress for it.

You will be aware by now that the British do not dress as Americans do, but the exact differences may elude you for some time.

HAIL TO BRITISH TWEEDS!

You have always associated two things, above all, with England—tea and tweeds. Back in America, you nursed along your favorite tweeds, just to bring with you, and you may even have bought a choice suit or jacket before leaving, to last until you could buy real, native British tweeds.

You have always pictured yourself Somewhere in England, swathed in a matted underbrush of Harris and Shetland.

During your first weeks in London you will go wild buying tweed suits and coats galore, of a quality that delights you, and at prices that seem ridiculous. Your wife may do the same thing, and you will both feel that your clothing problems are solved forever.

This will not be quite the case.

HOW TO DRESS IN TOWN

For your first important meeting in London you will dress carefully in your newest and most beautiful tweed suit, with knees lined in silk, a gay and expensive tattersall check shirt, and your finest hand-made Scotch-grain brogues. You will wish the fellows in the office back home could see you, all turned out like a proper English gentleman.

The British will notice you, too.

"Oh, I say, Brash, you Americans *do* have a delightful sense of humor!"

You will wonder how he knew, since you haven't said anything funny. You will notice that the other men, too, will look at you as though you were something special. You may, indeed, be so pleased with the impression you are creating that you will fail to note that every other man is wearing a stiff-collared white shirt, a smooth black worsted suit, and plain black laced oxfords with straight tips.

If any American is present, he may take you aside later:

"Uh, Buck, that sure is a beautiful tweed suit!"

"Glad you like it, Bill."

"I explained to the chaps that you were just going shooting, and——"

"Me, Bill? No!"

"Uh, they've got a kinda funny thing about tweeds, here, in town, I mean. Any old suit, as long as it's black, Buckley."

After this you will not wear tweeds in London again.

HOW TO DRESS IN THE COUNTRY

You will find a brisk social life clicking away in the country houses all around you. You will be invited often to "come over for a drink" by your fine English neighbors, the first time, perhaps, at an hour that may seem unusual to you, at about noon on Sunday. This is a favorite time for cocktail parties.

"You think I'm over-dressing a bit, Peg? It's only across the field and through the trees. Maybe just the wool sport shirt will be enough."

"Really? I thought I'd wear a cocktail dress and a fur coat."

"I'll go all-out, then. Shirt, tie, the good flannel

"The gardener is here to be paid off."

slacks, polished moccasins, and the number one tweed jacket. Nothing like tweeds in the country, Peg!"

You will be met at the door by your hostess, who may turn and call to her husband:

"Oh, Geoffrey, the gardener is here to be paid off—"

"No, really, I——"

"Goodness, I'm so sorry. You're the new Americans! My, you do look nice and out-doorsy!"

(The British are always polite.)

You will discover that all the men there, who also came across the field, or through the trees (some by Jaguar or Mini-Minor) are dressed in stiff-collared white shirts, smooth black worsted suits, and plain black laced oxfords with straight tips.

No one will express displeasure at the odd way you are dressed. You will, in fact, be praised:

"I say, Brash, you do look *comfortable*!"

Your wife, who has come in a full-length coat, has taken it off, and is left in a silk dress:

"Are you quite all right, my dear?"

"Oh, y-y-yes, f-f-fine, thank you!"

(She will be turning a light blue. The temperature in the living room, called lounge, will be an invigorating 54, with a light breeze blowing. All the other women will be wearing heavy woolen dresses, and many of them fur stoles. Stoles, in England, are for indoors.)

"My, you Americans are certainly warm blooded. I'd be simply *frozen* in a summer dress like that."

HOW TO DRESS FOR GARDENING

You will soon discover that in England tweeds are for digging in the garden, or for "shooting". Not "hunting": this is done on a horse, in a pink coat. It is safe to wear tweeds any place where you used to wear an old sweatshirt, or blue jeans.

BE FORMAL

For all occasions other than sports which require special costumes, such as the white of tennis or cricket, you are safe if you follow this rule: dress as you would for an informal funeral and you will be correct and inconspicuous everywhere. No need to wear a black necktie; colors are permitted, within certain bounds, as we shall see below.

A good, sturdy black suit, made of excellent British worsted, of a weight Americans use for winter overcoats, will see you through thick and thin, keep you warm, and last far longer than any other suit you have ever owned. It will rarely need pressing.

When the suit grows old, replace it with another just like it. The old one will become your sport clothes. Still later the trousers, which are indestructible, can be stuffed into your Wellingtons (rubber boots) and used as dungarees.

THE ALL-PURPOSE AIR TRAVELER'S WARDROBE

Because of the miracle of the black suit, it is possible to travel anywhere in Britain (or, indeed, to come here on a visit of considerable length) with only a briefcase, and be dressed adequately for everything but hunting and cricket.

What to wear: the suit, with stiff-collared white shirt, and black laced oxfords with straight tips. Wear a heavy cardigan or pullover under the suit. In other countries this can be carried over the arm. Wear, or carry, a warm raincoat, or Mac, preferably mud-colored, and dirty. If it is clean, rub it in any dirt or soot that is handy, or walk over it for a few minutes with dirty shoes. (See below.) During autumn, winter, and spring, long heavy underwear is advised.

What to carry in your briefcase: just carry an extra shirt or two, with several collars (stiff), an extra pair or two of socks (black), an extra pair of long underwear, a pair of sheep-lined slippers (no need to bring any, the best can be bought here) and a dressing gown (the bath will be down the hall).

Your hosts will lend you Wellingtons; in a pinch these can be bought for a few shillings.

"SHOULD I GO TO A TAILOR?"

The answer is, yes, you should. You may always have been fitted adequately by ready-made (in British, "off-the-peg") clothes in the States, but you will be disappointed in England:

"Well, the color is a lovely, mournful black, Buckley, but there's this funny dent in your back."

"Where?"

"It runs from *here*—"

"That tickles."

"—diagonally down to *here*. Didn't they adjust the shoulders?"

You will find that the number of sizes is small, and

the alterations only for waist, sleeve, and trouser length. They will rarely re-shape shoulders, or do anything else that is complicated.

On the other hand, you don't need to be told about British made-to-measure.

You know perfectly well that you have no real structural faults, yourself. But for some reason, no one has ever appreciated how manly a figure you have. A British tailor will simply make this apparent.

"You do look just lovely, Buckley. What on *earth* did they do with your tummy?"

"It's this active, hard-living British life, Peg."

"Just don't go back to that rich-living, pot-bellied other suit, Buckley."

In America, France, and indeed in most other countries, it is the women who look well-dressed, and the men who look mouse-like and shabby.

You will note that in England the reverse is true. English men look like peacocks—*even though they are dressed largely in black.*

"Well, Buckley, just because you *look* like one of the Grenadier Guards, don't think *I'm* going to slink into a sweater and skirt!"

It is wise to remember that Paris is now only two hours away.

HOW TO WEAR A TIE WITHOUT BECOMING A BOUNDER

American males have long felt that one of Britain's greatest contributions to civilization was the regimental stripe necktie, suitable for most occasions, colorful without being gaudy, timeless, and capable of infinite variety.

You have probably nursed along a cherished collection of a few dozen of them, in color combinations to match every outfit.

Leave them *all* at home.

No matter what combination of diagonal stripes you wear, they will be sure to attract others of their kind:

"Oh, I say! Platterhouse!"

(Or, "Gad! Twelfth Devonian Fusiliers!")

"Beg your pardon?"

"Platterhouse!"

(You will notice by this time that he is wearing a tie just like yours, and pointing at your neck.)

"Well, actually, no, I'm not, I, uh——"

"You mean you're—you're *not* Platter-house?"

(You will wish you were Platterhouse, or that you could remove it from your neck.)

On this island, all diagonally striped neckties are banners, and standards. If you wear one you may become a rallying point.

There is no law that says you can't wear an Old Platterhouse tie, any more than there is one saying you can't wear a Yale "Y", willy-nilly. But you will be a bounder.

Plain colors, horizontal or vertical stripes, or paisley designs are all safe. Indeed, no regiment, old school, or club will object to hand-painted nudes, day-glo colors, or ties wired for flashing lights or funny noises, but these will place you outside the scope of this volume.

She can do it and watch television.

SWEATERS ARE A WAY OF LIFE

When the Romans left, and took the central heating with them, life was not possible again in Britain until the invention of the sweater.

Everyone wears a sweater, all the time. You may not see it, but it is there.

Everywhere you look, women are knitting. In America, the lower-priced women's magazines are devoted largely to cooking, home-making, and sex-in-marriage. In England they are full of instructions for knitting sweaters. No one knows why this is true, because there is a huge chain of stores devoted almost entirely to the sale of sweaters, at prices that seem lower than the cost of the wool. One theory is that the English feel guilty about sitting down, unless they are doing several things at once.

Almost anything a British housewife can do in a sitting or reclining position she can do and knit at the same time. She can do it and watch television, play bingo, or mind the baby. Marriage counsellors, indeed, allege that the versatility of young knitting wives knows almost no bounds. Few figures are available on this, and independently conducted experiments are often fruitless:

"Buckley, all I can say is—it must take a lot of practice. Now, turn out the light, will you, Love?"

As you might expect, the word "sweater" (scarcely genteel!) has been refined, or U-Upped, almost out of existence. There has been little sweat since Sir Winston's, though people still perspire freely. Sweaters have become, variously, cardigans, pull-overs, jumpers, or woolies.

WHERE TO BE DIRTY

You will be able to spot an Englishman anywhere by his raincoat. It will be dirty. If it is not dirty he will get it dirty. It is like the Ivy League and white buck shoes, which had to be dirty before they could be worn in public. (This grew until it covered tennis shoes, too. To this day you can tell English tennis players from Americans; the English tennis shoes will be carefully whitened, the American ones carefully soiled.)

Old grey flannel trousers, called "bags", have to be dirty in England, too. If your wife has yours cleaned, by mistake, you will have to soil them again before wearing.

And before you forget it, write down now that "pants" always mean underpants. What you wear out in the open are trousers. Mistakes in this area can lead to nasty misunderstandings.

WHAT ABOUT RAIN?

There are three more things you must know about raincoats:

1. They are called "Macs", whether or not they are made by Macintosh, as in a "plastic Mac".

2. The collars are never turned up, no matter how hard it is raining.

3. Most men don't wear them, they carry umbrellas, furled, even when it is raining. The British attitude toward rain is to pretend that it isn't.

WHAT TO TELL YOUR BARBER

You will be delighted to discover that haircuts in England are only about fifty cents, saving you more than a dollar a crop.

Your first inclination is to have as many as possible, to multiply the savings. You will be sorry you cannot have several at once, or send some home to your friends.

It is wise to control this urge. A Briton is not really "U" if one can see the tops of his ears. His locks are long and flowing. In any active sport he will have to restrain them with a cap, hair ribbon, or knotted handkerchief in order to see out.

You will not want to go this far, but some Americans meet the British half way with a mildly shaggy look.

If you are going to have a defiantly American crew cut, train your barber carefully.

"Heavens, Buckley! You look like the King of Siam!"

"We had a long talk about it afterward, Peg. Next time he'll leave some hair on the sides. Very good barber, really."

A crew cut will give you, in British eyes, a startled, or slightly frightened expression, and will set you apart. You will be given ice in your drinks without asking for it. Decide for yourself how much these things mean to you.

ARE DERBIES FOR EVERYONE?

The hat that Charlie Chaplin made famous is *not* called a derby in Britain, and if it were it would be pronounced "darby". It is a bowler, and it is not for you.

Bowlers were given to officers, after the war. They have been trying to wear them out, ever since. Some have succeeded in getting them a little green, but no one has worn one out, and you will still see them everywhere.

You can buy new ones, and some Americans do. Do not try to buy a brown or grey one. Like suits, they come in black. The first time you put one on it will feel like wearing a chamber pot. It would feel like a chamber pot the second and third times, also, but before this happens social pressures will be applied by wives, children, and fellow Americans. You will then put it away with all the tweed suits. It will not feel comfortable in this company, but never mind.

Everyone wears bowlers in the Wall Street of London, called The City. They will let you in without one, but everyone will know you are just visiting.

Some Americans wear homburgs, but most wear nothing at all. You will wonder why this is so, until you wear your normal American snap-brim:

"Oh, my, Mr. Brash, what a lovely *trilby*!"

You will see she is looking at your hat. You will feel, somehow, that you have been caught in public wearing curl papers or a snood. Your snap-brim will never seem the same again.

Your head, like that of most Americans in England, will be bare, cool at times, lashed by rain, and whipped by wind. But bare.

THE FOUR STAGES OF DRESS

Every American male living in England goes through these phases of dress:

1. **The opening, or tweed, phase**
2. **The secondary, or "look British" phase,**

in which you hide all your American brown and light grey suits, and wear only your navy blue suit, and the new British black one.

3. **The rebound, Re-Assert Americanism, or Yankee Doodle phase**

This is most common among those engaged in any industry in which Americans are believed to have mystic or superhuman powers, like advertising or plumbing. Often men who are considered quite stupid in the States are listened to with awe and wonder, as we shall see in a later chapter. In any case, if it is worth money to you to *be* an American, you may want to *look* like one. In this phase, pull out your old light-colored suits, slip-on shoes, brightly patterened shirts, and assertive ties. Some go so far as to wear a *different* old school tie every day for a month. This is good only if you are in a position of great power.*

---

* It is in this phase that your children, too, may revert to cowboy suits, and your wife to toreador pants, or whatever American fad she remembers best.

4. Final, or rich-country-gentleman phase,

in which you really don't give a damn. Wear eccentric combinations of British clothes, like tan cavalry twill trousers and navy blue brass-buttoned blazer, suede shoes, and knotted scarf or cravat instead of necktie.

A WORD TO WOMEN

There is no use trying to advise women in a reference work of this kind, since anything said about women's fashions today would not be true tomorrow.

Just one word of relatively permanent advice: leave your Bermuda shorts at home.

Many women ask: "If it is really too cool to wear cottons in summer, should I bring them anyway?" The answer is, yes, you should. They *do* wear cotton in summer, though of course they wear a heavy sweater on top.

*   *   *   *

Meanwhile, you will be completely surrounded by British weather, and you had better learn how to cope with it.

10

How to Make the Worst of the Weather

ENGLISH WEATHER will come as a great surprise to you. You will have to learn how to make the worst of it.

If you have lived in almost any state except Florida or California, you will think you have come to a health resort.

You are accustomed to sweltering and almost dying every summer from 95 degree heat and high humidity. "Shall I," you ask, "bring air conditioners, electric fans, and iced tea spoons?" No, not to England, where summers are like those in northern Maine. You will sleep under blankets every night, all summer, and wear a wool suit every day, and soon be as shocked as the British when the papers say: "Heat wave! Temperatures to soar into the seventies!"

You will discover, on a globe, that your latitude is the same as Hudson Bay. You will then understand the cool summers, and wonder if you should buy a parka for an arctic winter.

This will not be the case, either. The average British winter will seem to you like a mild autumn. Even the coldest winter will seem pleasant to you, with temperatures rarely going below 20.

NEVER LET THEM KNOW

After reading the above paragraphs, tear them out neatly from the book and burn them. Do not let the British know that you know. They are firmly convinced they have the worst weather in the world. Nothing will change their minds.

It is a social error in Britain to praise the weather.

Let us say it is late September. You are in your ground floor flat, your children are in school everywhere, your black suit is in the wardrobe, the sun is shining brightly in the garden, and the michaelmas daisies are in full bloom. You will think all is right with the world. You greet your neighbor, a pleasant chap who lives in a flat upstairs:

"Well, Mr. Price-Johnson, lovely day, isn't it?"

"Good afternoon, Mr. Brash!"

(You may feel you know him quite well by now, but in England one doesn't rush the Christian names.)

"Beautiful sunshine, isn't it?"

"Actually, you know, it's the worst autumn in a hundred and fifty-six years. Read it in the paper last night."

(The papers can always prove, by statistics, that the current season is the worst in 156 years.)

"Uh—seemed quite pleasant to me, Mr Price-Johnson."

(He will begin to look at you, for the first time since you've known him, with an air of polite hostility.)

"Shocking, actually."

In all periods of beautiful weather you will note that tensions are beginning to build, and tempers flare. Just before the breaking point, it will begin to sprinkle, or the temperature drop to 45, or some equivalent disaster, and the British will close ranks once more against the common enemy:

"Shocking, isn't it, Mr. Price-Johnson?"

"Simply shocking, Mr. Brash! Worst weather in the world!"

"Absolutely, Mr. Price-Johnson!"

(He will be smiling happily, and you will know he is once more your friend.)

WATCH THE CALENDAR

As the temperature drops you will rejoice that you live in the warmest house for miles around.

"B–Buckley, I'm frozen!"

"Put on a sweater. Peg."

"I've got on *two* sweaters now. It's fifty in here! Can't you *do* something?"

"I've talked to the agent twice. Absolutely no heat until October first."

"No matter *how* cold it is?"

Until October first you will all move into the kitchen, where the coal stove will keep things nice and warm.

THE WEATHER AND THE CLASS WAR

The weather is the only thing the British classes have in common. In America, where class differences are almost as strong, though less permanent, there are a number of other meeting points. You may say to the elevator man or the taxi driver:

"How about that? A no–hitter going into the ninth!"

(You can always pick tid-bits like this out of the paper without actually knowing who is playing.)

"Yeah, I tole ya he was gonna moider 'em!"

This establishes *rapport*, and democracy marches on. In England, however, not even the same sports are common to all the classes, as we shall see later.

The weather is all that is left. It serves not only to show friendliness, *but also to establish class immediately.*

"Beastly, isn't it?"

(This is always good, no matter what the weather is.)

"Blimey, 'orrible, sir!"

Without ever having seen each other before, class relationship is established in little over two seconds.

WHAT TO DO ABOUT WINTER

One day you will hear that there will be "two degrees of frost". This means the temperature is going down to thirty degrees. Everywhere you look you will see worried faces. Warnings will come over the radio. Headlines will read: BIG FREEZE.

You will laugh gaily to yourself, not knowing what is in store:

"Buckley, come quickly! It's Pete, in the billiard room!"

"I can't sleep, Daddy. It's too hot!"

"And all that hissing and clanging, Buckley. It must be eighty in here!"

"Well, that's a switch."

"Especially since it's now forty-eight in the bedroom."

"I'll turn off the radiators."

"They won't *turn* off."

"He's right over the furnace. They must have turned up the heat."

"We'll open the doors, Pete."

It will not be over. Soon there will be four degrees of frost! Twenty-eight above zero! Headlines read: ARCTIC BRITAIN! and ICE AGE ARRIVES!

Everyone will look grim and tense. No good showing them your Paris *Herald*, which says it was fifteen below zero in Minneapolis, three below zero in Chicago, and six above in New York.

You will wonder why everyone is so alarmed.

"Buckley, I thought you'd *never* get home! There's no water for the sink! The pipes are frozen!"

"Impossible! It's at least fifty-five in here!"

"The pipes run outside the house—out there!"

"Why?"

"Everybody's do. I can't wash the dishes!"

"Get a kettle. We'll bring some from the bathroom."

"But it won't run out, either—the drain is frozen, too!"

You will try to get a plumber, and he will tell you there are a hundred people ahead of you. Everybody else's pipes are frozen, too.

"Oh, Daddy, it snowed last night! Isn't that smashing?"

(They will be picking up strange words at school.)

"Smashing. Gosh, a little bit did stick. Three or four inches."

The entire nation will be in a state of emergency. Headlines read: TRAFFIC CHAOS! Train service is disrupted, roads blocked by skidding vehicles, food deliveries halted. Helicopters are dropping hay to sheep.

"Home at last, Peg! Took me three hours! Did Sally's train get through?"

"Her school's cancelled. So is Pete's. Lavatories frozen! I might add—so are ours."

"Have a drink of water, Daddy? A man brought it in a truck."

"Mr Price-Johnson was saying, Buckley, that our coal supply is almost gone. They're going to turn off the central heating."

"Get out the electric heater."

"They just said on the radio that the power is being cut, too."

"What's that thing?"

"A paraffin heater. Kerosene to you, Buckley. Mr. Price-Johnson only had two—but he loaned us one."

In just a few weeks, however, the wind will change,

Water will flow once again.

the thaw will come, and the water will flow once again:

"Buckley, there's a flood in the bedroom!"

"I was upstairs, Daddy. Mr. Price-Johnson said not to worry. It's happening to everybody."

"It's how they tell which pipes got busted by the ice, Buckley—when they thaw out."

HOW TO GUARD AGAINST SPRING

Before many more days pass, the plumbers will come and the floods will recede. Soon the crocuses will pop out, and the daffodils, and the apple blossoms. New-born lambs will be gambolling on the meadows. And because of the Green Belt system, you won't have to drive for hours to see all this. It will be going on all around you.

You will be in the middle of your first English spring. They have them every year, and are used to them.

This is a time of grave social danger. Guard against any tendency to be ecstatic, or to babble happily to your British neighbors. They will not thank you for it.

You will not be able to say "beastly!" or "shocking" about the weather *immediately* at hand, but happily you can draw on the past for some time:

"Shocking, wasn't it, Mr. Price-Johnson?"

"Absolutely shocking, Mr. Brash! Worst winter in a hundred and thirty-eight years!"

LET THE RADIO HELP YOU

If good weather continues, the horrors of the past will begin to recede. Once again tensions will rise and tempers flare. It will be up to you to restore sanity.

Let the radio be your ally. In England it is almost

impossible to discover what your local weather is going to be. Every weather forecast takes five minutes, and covers in meticulous detail the Orkney Islands, the Shetlands, East Anglia, Wales, Northern Ireland, and Scotland.

"Did he say fog, Buckley?"

"I thought that was for the Shetland Islands."

"Weren't they having gale force winds?"

"That was East Anglia."

"Where is East Anglia, anyway?"

"East Anglia, Father, is the area south of the Wash, including——"

"Thank you, Pete. Later, please?"

"I'm sure he said bright intervals."

"He always says bright intervals."

"I'll bring my plastic mac."

At first you may wonder how this can serve your purposes. Then you will discover that all Britons are just as confused by this as you are. They long ago turned off their ears, and have given up trying to make any sense out of it.

This will help you to bring sunshine, in a manner of speaking, into the lives of your British friends:

"Good morning, Mr. Price-Johnson!"

"Good morning, Mr. Brash!"

(The sun is shining brightly, the scent of blossoms is in the air. He is desolate.)

"May look all right now—but did you hear the forecast for the Frisian Islands?"

"Well—I had it on——"

"Isobars dropping like a shot! People blowing off the pavement! May be here by sundown, Mr. Price-Johnson!"

"You don't say, Mr. Brash!"

(His eyes will begin to brighten, and his old smile return. You will have made his day.)

A few other phrases you can use are: "Anti-cyclone brewing over the Orkneys!" or: "Hill-fog in the Pennines—and you know what that can lead to!"

Once you have learned to make the weather work for you, you will be able to face other, more complicated tasks.

11

"Are We Really SAFE Here?"

WHEN YOU first land in England you will not be frightened at all. Everywhere you look you will see mild and gentle people. You will think they would never hurt a fly.

You will feel that you are far safer here than you used to be when you were home in bed.

After a while, this feeling will begin to disappear. You will wonder whether the British are really what they seem.

MURDER IS AN INDOOR SPORT

Let us say it is a cold night in early spring. A bit of fog lingers in the air. The hour is late, and you are alone in the living room, reading.

You hear a knock, and go to the door:

"Oh. Hope I didn't give you a turn, Mr. Brash!"

"No, I'll be all right in a minute, Mr. Price-Johnson."

"I know it is late to call, but I just finished this book, and I did want to return it."

"Like to borrow something else? New American novel?"

"That's very good of you, but——"

(He will look at you in an eerie manner.)

"—what I'm really interested in, Mr. Brash, is—eh-heh—murder!"

Nothing more will happen—*then*—but your suspicions will be aroused.

"Buckley, I wish you hadn't told me that about Mr. Price-Johnson——"

"Not to worry, Peg!"

(Your speech may be getting a bit British, too.)

"Well, ever since, he has looked a bit suspicious."

This will not end it. Once alerted, you will begin to see ominous signs everywhere.

Let us say you are planning an evening at the theatre, with long-established London Americans:

"Well, we've got a nice choice, Buckley. This play is a single murder, this other one is a double, and in this one you've got *three* corpses."

"Does it *have* to be murder?"

"Well, Buck, there are basically two kinds of plays in London now, murder and bicycle factory."

"Let's try the bicycles."

"Frankly, I don't think you're ready for that yet, Buck."

You will find you are not yet prepared for serious plays, which are written in Northern Talk, which will sound to you, at first, like grunts and *oooops*. For the first few years you will not understand a word the actors say.

Remember this simple rule: if the actors wear neckties, the play will be about murder. At first, these will be the only plays you can understand. And you will feel, even more, that you are surrounded by perpetual premeditated homicide.

Murder, you will discover, is the everyday pastime of the British middle classes.

"SHOULD I SEEK PROTECTION?"

Some Americans, their nerves worn thin, run in terror to the police.

This is not necessary. In England, the police *will come to you.*

BEWARE OF ALIENS

The first thing to remember is to keep calm:

"Peg, as I left this morning, I thought I saw a police woman going toward our flats."

"I talked to her. She was looking for aliens."

"Gosh—are there *aliens* lurking around here, too?"

"Yes, Buckley. *Us.*"

Every American knows that he cannot be an alien. You know it, too. Aliens are foreigners. They are somebody else. (The British also know that they can never be aliens, either, no matter where *they* are.)

The police, however, will make the mistake of considering you an alien. It will be their duty to control you.

The way they do this is with rubber stamps. You may not think you can control people with rubber stamps, but you can.

They will make you buy a little green book which has nothing in it but your picture, and you will have to give them that. It will have plenty of blank pages for rubber stamps. Every few months you will have to go to the police station and be controlled. Various people there will look at the book, and call you "Sir", and not "Hey, Mac", the way policemen sometimes do in the States. They will stamp the book, and you will be able to go back home.

In between being controlled at the station, they will send around a police girl on a bicycle to control you at home. Most of them are young and pretty, in snappy uniforms. The police girl will call you "Sir", too, and look at the stamps in the book. She will never stamp it, just look, say "Thank you, sir", and go away. You will wish she could stay longer, but she never does.

You will think at first they are just making sure you have not been murdered yet.

You will wish she could stay longer.

THE REAL TRUTH ABOUT
BRITISH MURDER

After a long spell of being frightened you will discover the real truth about murder in Britain.

Murder is a parlor game because they don't believe it is real.

Regular, every-day murder, in the American sense, hardly exists in England at all. There are about 500 murders every year in New York City, and about 40 a year in London.

Where murder is commonplace, it loses its charm. A *real* murder is untidy, like cleaning fish, or throwing up. John Dickson Carr once said: "No one is ever really killed in the library." In England, murder is for the library.

Be frightened all you want, in a nice, cozy, literary way. You have never been safer in your life.

GUNS ARE FOR GROUSE

You are likely to be shot only if you get between an Englishman and a grouse. This will happen only during the season, between mid-August and mid-December.

The English hardly ever shoot each other on purpose. They have agreed among themselves not to, even in the course of normal, workaday crime.

Everyone knows that British policemen, or "Bobbies", do not carry guns. But it goes much farther than that.

One day in December, 1961, a band of eight men, in two large trucks, attacked a payroll car carrying £125,000, or about $350,000. It was a well-planned professional job. The bandits pulled off the armored car's door with grappling hooks attached to one of the trucks. Inside,

with the money, were an unarmed policeman, a dog, and two bank guards. The robbers were armed with wooden pick handles, toy guns that couldn't shoot, and pepper to throw in the eyes of the guards; in short, they were conventionally armed for this sort of job.

Everything was going smoothly, and the bandits were getting the money, when suddenly one of the guards broke the rules of the game. He drew a *real, loaded* .22 calibre pistol and *shot it*, slightly wounding one of the bandits.

Everyone present was shocked.

"He has a real gun!" one of the bandits said.

"That isn't fair!" said one of the others, and they all left, without taking the money.

"He has a real gun!"

The British public was up in arms, not because a payroll had been threatened, but because a guard had broken the rules and used a real gun. Would there be an arms race? Would bandits actually start using guns themselves? Should the guards be armed, too, with toy guns and pepper? Would crossbows of the latest design be considered unfair? A sword or two wielded by stout fellows in close-fitting goggles might have created a veritable carnage—but everyone felt that this, after all, was just the thing they were trying to avoid.

The situation had not changed at all two years later, when the Great Train Robbery occurred. A mail train was halted and robbed of more than two million pounds, or about six million dollars.

When asked why the many guards were powerless to stop this, the authorities said: "But the robbers were armed!"

When you have reached the stage at which you are outraged by a bank guard's carrying a .22 pistol to guard $350,000 or a post office guard's carrying a six-shooter to save six million, then you can truly say you are at home in the British Isles.

RESPECT THE THIN RED, OR DARK GREY, LINE

Once you have begun to feel really safe, you will dare to join the British queues, pronounced "cues".

"What is a queue, Daddy?" your children will ask, at first. The answer is not as simple as it seems.

In some countries they have mobs and riots. In England they have queues.

A queue is a group of people waiting in line. But in England it is far, far more than that. Queues are a way of life.

Everyone knows that the British Empire was built by the thin red line of the British infantry, against which most of the undeveloped people of the world (and quite a few developed ones) hurled themselves, to no avail.

"Why," you may ask, "did the thin red line never break?" Because of courage, of course. However, it was also because the soldiers thought they were in a queue.

Today the queue is no longer red. It is more likely to be mouse-colored, or black, but its character is unchanged. Whenever two or more Britons come together, they form a queue. Often they do not know what the queue is for. The important thing is to get one's place in it *first*, and then find out what it is for. One's place will *always* be inviolate. A British queue *never* breaks.

You may hear one Briton, who has been standing in a queue with you for twenty minutes or so, ask another (he has delayed all this time, summoning up courage to speak to someone he has not "met"):

"Ah, pardon me, can you tell me what this queue is for?"

"Actually, no. Had meant to pop up front and ask. Afraid to lose my place, you know. Shouldn't be much longer before we're there."

You will find there are three major types of queue:

1. The ordinary, or primary, type queue,

in which people simply stand in line, waiting. One of the most numerous is the bus queue. Sometimes these can form complex patterns, as suggested by signs: "Queue this side for Waterloo ... Queue other side for beyond Waterloo." Bus queues differ in one respect only from other queues; the queue-ers remain motionless and orderly for minutes, even hours at a time, no one stepping an inch out of line *until the bus arrives*, when it instantly dissolves into a surging mob, converging on the bus.

2. Mental queues.

These are people "in" a queue but not actually *standing* in it. Their places exist only *in the mind*, but are equally inviolable. For example, in a baker's shop, too small for a regular queue, women waiting for bread will form a mental queue in the exact order in which they entered the shop.

3. Pre-queue queues.

Sometimes numbers are assigned to people, to give them the security of *being* in a queue without actually standing up, or having your queue and eating it, too. A Briton is never *really* happy unless he is in some queue, and an arrangement like this gives him the chance to be in two queues at once, a heady experience indeed. However, there has to be an orderly, queue-ey way to obtain the numbers, so it will be necessary to queue for queue numbers, hence the pre-queue queue.

*   *   *   *

With your safety assured, and your place in the queues secure, you will feel that the police are your friends, and that you are in no danger of running foul of the law. This, however, may not be the case, as we shall see directly.

12

Now for the Open Road!

NEVER BE A RESIDENT

TRY TO remember that all countries, including England, have split personalities about motorists. They all believe there are two kinds, tourists and residents. The tourists are the good motorists, who can do no wrong. The residents are the bad ones.

Try to be a tourist as long as you can. Never be a resident until they *make* you be one.

The amount of trouble they went to, just to get you to drive in, would amaze you. They have been trying for *years* to get you to come. They established offices in every major city in the world; they spent millions in advertising, printing folders, maps, and publicity stories by the ton. Little by little they abolished all the frontier difficulties, threw out the triptychs and *carnets de passage* for the car, and the visas for you. Every country became like a drive-in store, with the doors wide open. Drive right in and bring your money and your car with you.

As long as you are a tourist, nothing is too good for you.

Suddenly something will snap. You will be the same. You will still be spending your money, still paying them 38¢ a gallon tax, on every gallon of petrol, still benefitting the economy and improving their balance of payments, making them richer by the day.

But suddenly the clock will strike twelve and you will be a resident. Beware!

REMEMBER YOUR DRIVING LICENSE

By this time you will have been driving in England for more than a year. Gone are your days of terror on the road. You will wonder how you could have been so frightened. Roundabouts will at last seem like friendly, social gatherings. You will be used to missing cars coming at you head-on by an inch or two.

You will no longer be a menace to life and limb, but a seasoned driver, tried and tested on the most difficult roads in the world. You will be experienced, safe, and considerate.

This is the time they have been waiting for.

"Oh, Buckley, the funniest thing happened to me in London, today! I made some stupid turn into a one-way street, and the policeman wanted to see my driving license—and guess what! Our New York driving licenses expired two months ago. We have to go right away and get provisional licenses."

Almost anyone over 17 can get a provisional license, by simply filling out a form and paying ten shillings, or $1.40:

"There you are, sir."

"Fine, thanks. That's all I need to drive, is it?"

"Yes, sir. Is that your car, sir?"

"Yes."

"If you have no other valid license, sir, you'll have to put 'L' plates on it——"

"'*L*' *plates?*"

"For 'learner', sir."

"I've been driving for more than twenty years—including more than a year in England!"

"You'll have to use 'L' plates, sir, unless you pass your driving test."

"Okay, I'll get the plates."

"But you can't drive this car now, sir, even with the 'L' plates. A learner-driver must be accompanied, in the vehicle, by a fully licensed driver——"

"I can't even get my own car *home*?"

"Perhaps we could help you with that, sir."

"But my wife has a provisional license, too. Can't we even drive—together?"

"Not unless you have a licensed driver with you, sir."

"I want to take my driving test tomorrow!"

"Sorry, sir, there's quite a waiting list. It may take several months."

Do not worry. You will not need a license to ride a bicycle, unless there is any kind of motor on it. They will let you cycle everywhere, and in any weather:

"Hey, Mom, make Dad stop playing with my bike in the rain!"

"Daddy is *not* playing. He's practising."

"Make him get his own bike!"

"He is. And so am I."

A few months of pedalling will do wonders for you, and give you a tolerance for bicycles you never had before:

"Now this great big Morris Minor was bearing down on me, Peg, but I held steady, see, and I——"

"Isn't Daddy *brave*?"

Meanwhile, everyone will try to persuade you to go to a driving school.

"Well, *I* am, Buckley. They say not one person in *ten* can pass without special instruction."

"I've driven since I was fourteen! And in 44 states and 11 countries in Europe!"

After you fail your first test, you will have to wait two or three months for your next one. All your licensed friends will try to give you instruction:

"It's all right, you can drive with *me*, Buckley. Let me tie on your 'L' plates."

"Just because *you* had an easy examiner, Peg!"

"Today we'll just practice arm signals. You have to hold out your arm every time you pass everything."

"Even bicycles?"

"Especially bicycles. You have to drive one-handed most of the time."

"Peg, *nobody* does all this when they're really driving."

"They do when they take the test!"

Do not be discouraged if you fail the second, or third, or fourth test. There is no limit to the number they will let you take. Many have tried it half a dozen times or more.

"I think a professional teacher would be better now, Buckley. You don't really believe what I tell you."

"It's just that I get more nervous now, every test!"

NEVER SAY DIE!

One day, though, you will pass the test, and you will be able to drive again, all by yourself, just as you did on your first day in England. For some weeks you will continue to wave your hands in the air when you pass bicycles or make turns, but after a while you will go back to the electric turn indicators, like everyone else.

You will be a fully licensed British driver. Take care!

13

"Do I WANT My Daughter to be a Duchess?"

Part II

LET US assume you have ignored all warnings, and still have your daughter living with you in England.

By this time your most desperate problem will be the dilemma of a university education:

"Buckley, I can't get anyone to even *believe* Susan's going to a university. None of the girls she knows is going to one."

"Mother, Barry *is* from Oxford!"

This will be true. Only one girl in a *hundred* goes to a university in England, and those who do are considered odd.

"Buckley, her headmistress says she hasn't one chance in twenty-five of getting into Oxford or Cambridge."

"What about some of the other universities?"

"You mean there *are* any others?"

Many Americans refuse to admit the existence of provincial universities, and those American mothers who do tend to regard them as matrimonial *cul de sacs*.

Even *before* she can enter any university, your daughter will encounter grave dangers:

"Susan, was that you I saw on the back end of that motorcycle?"

"That must have been Barry's, Father."

"And who is Barry?"

"He's the one I'm going to sit in Trafalgar Square with."

"That's what I mean, Buckley! Once you get away from the Oxford boys——"

"Mother, Barry *is* from Oxford!"

"And he's a beatnik and a sit-down communist?"

"Father, don't be antediluvian! Barry's a member of the Labor Party! He's often quite angry at the communists!"

Do not despair. Write quickly to the U.S. College Entrance Examination Board. They will send you all the details you need. Your daughter can take her American College Board exams right in London.

Your problems, however, will not be over.

14

How to Get Rich in England
Part I

THE MOMENT you land on these shores it will be assumed you are rich, by everyone except other Americans, who know better.

You may be several thousand dollars in debt, with payments still owed on a number of electrical appliances you don't even *have* any more, and with an interesting situation at the Income Tax Bureau which will force you to earn at least as much as you did the year before, just to stay the same amount behind.

But to the British you will seem to be *acting* rich, and that will be enough for them.

"DO I REALLY *WANT* TO GET RICHER?"

Everyone has told you that Americans are all crass materialists, and that Europeans are not.

You will wonder, then, whether you should really try to make more money, or whether you should just lie back and let the culture roll over you.

You will have a shocking surprise.

You will be amazed to discover that most Europeans, including the British, are far more materialistic than you. It is not at all mysterious when you think about it. For many years, up to now, Europeans haven't had enough material of any kind, and this naturally has concentrated their minds on it.

Many Americans—though by no means all—have had such a glut of material for so long that they have begun to think about something else.

Should you, then, give way to your growing desire to gather cerebral rosebuds, or should you join the New Europeans and just wade right up to the trough?

SET A LOFTY GOAL

While you are haggling over this question with your conscience, your wife will settle it for you:

"Oh, Buckley, I saw the most gorgeous Manor House in the whole world! And we can just *steal* it for fifteen——"

"Fifteen thousand pounds?"

"Of course it's just a *shell*, but that's the beauty of it. We can put in everything, just the way we want it. *Blazing* heat, *real* bathrooms, a *miracle* kitchen. We could do it all for another five."

"You are now up to fifty-six thousand dollars, Peg."

"You men are so *materialistic*. It's only money, isn't it?"

THE MONEY IS ALL AROUND

Luckily it is possible in England to get rich easily and quickly, without really putting your mind on it. You can do it without becoming *too* materialistic, and without too many niggling details.

It is much easier to do here than in America.

Just follow a few simple rules and then stand back, and get out of the way of the money.

START AT THE TOP

All Americans feel that the thing to do is to start at the bottom. They know it is possible to join the Mail Room, or find some other menial post and rise quickly to the top by force of character, and clarity of mind.

In England this is not quite possible. Here, great force of character and clarity of mind may get you to the top of the bottom, but rarely to the top.

In England it is best to start at the top. If you are very young, and know the right people, or talk the right way, they will start you at the bottom of the top, which is very different from the bottom. You will be made an "apprentice" or "trainee".

If you were an Englishman they would know right where to put you after looking at your tie, or hearing the first ten words.

If you are an American they cannot tell at all. The reason you will go to the top is because of the force of your character, the clarity of your mind, and because your home company owns fifty-one per cent of the stock.

Otherwise you may have a difficult time, unless you can pass yourself off as an expert at something Americans are supposed to know about, like electronic brains, merchandising, or teenage music.

THE BRITISH OFFICE CAN BE A HAPPY PLACE

You will soon realize that getting to the top is not enough, but while you are discovering this, you will also be learning the British way of life in business, so different from anything you have experienced before.

It can be happy and rewarding in many ways, once you have mastered the basic Office Code.

We have already learned not to wear tweeds in the office, but there is more to it than that.

HOW TO HANDLE AN ENGLISH SECRETARY

We all know that English secretaries are the best in the world. They are now becoming one of Britain's major exports to America, rivalling sport cars and Scotch whiskey.

No need to import them here! They are all around, and can be obtained everywhere at modest cost. Unlike British biscuits, the best ones are not always sent abroad. Many first-rate and lovely ones are kept right at home.

When you see your new secretary, the chances are you will be delighted.

"Miss Mainwaring will be your secretary, Mr. Brash."

"How wonderful! I mean—how do you do, Miss Mainwaring. Where are they going to put you?"

"Well, right here, I think."

"Oh? Then they're moving me next door?"

"No, I think you'll be right here with me, Mr. Brash."

You will be accustomed to the American outside-secretary system, with the girl outside your office, in the hall. The British way is much more intimate. In England your secretary is often your room-mate. (It should be added here that your own office is usually called your "room", as in: "Why don't we have the meeting in my room.")

The new American, noting this room-mate custom, and the habit, discussed in a moment, of keeping office

The best ones are not always sent abroad.

doors *closed*, leaps to conclusions which seldom have basis in fact.

The object is not intimacy, or Getting to Know Your Secretary Better. It is simply to keep her warm. She cannot sit, as American secretaries do, in the corridor, because a fifteen to twenty knot wind will be blowing out there, and the temperature will be close to a light frost.

It is not *you* she wants to be near, but your electric fire.

No need, then for you to buzz or shout for your secretary. She will be right there, no matter what. This leads to a peculiarly British phenomenon, which requires separate discussion.

105

THE PHENOMENON OF THE WANDERING, OR LOST, SECRETARY

Many times during the course of a rough-and-tumble business day, matters will arise that are not for the ears of a growing girl. You may have to scold a subordinate, entertain an interesting offer, play company politics, illustrate a point by telling a rough anecdote, or make other attempts to improve your position in a sensitive, or confidential manner.

Each time you will have to say:

"Miss Mainwaring, would you please get me some cigarettes?"

She will know you have plenty of cigarettes, and that you wish to be left alone. She will throw on an extra cardigan and go off with a brave smile into the hallways.

If she walks briskly she will keep warm, and she is sure to have company. Many other temporarily unwanted girls will be there, too, aimlessly pacing the corridors, the wind whistling in their ears.

You will see them walking up and down in every British office, often tired, but sometimes pink-cheeked and hearty. Sometimes they lose their way and must ask others where you are. Do not try to find them. They will come back, in time.

KEEP YOUR MIND OPEN

One of the glories of America is the open mind. You have always prided yourself on *your* open mind, though you suspect that in some other Americans the statement: "I have an open mind about it", may be another way of saying: "I don't know anything about it, don't have time to learn, and if I did I wouldn't want to offend anyone by taking any definite view about it, and please don't quote me."

You have always lived in an open society, where faces are open, hearts are open, and heads are open. As a symbol of this, office doors are kept open, too.

American business is based solidly on the open door policy. Your open office door means you are available to everyone, sociable, and democratic. You are "the kind of guy who works with all us other guys".

In practice, of course, you have a secretary sitting outside your open door to keep everyone out.

In England, all this is different.

KEEP YOUR DOOR CLOSED

The British will allow you to keep your mind open, as long as you keep your door closed.

Office doors in England are always kept tightly closed, except when people are going in or out. They are closed again as quickly as possible. You do not need to lock them.

This does not indicate closed minds. Not necessarily. You close the door simply because it is cold out in the hall.

HOW TO GET A DRINK OF WATER

The knottiest problem facing Americans in English offices is: how to get a drink of water.

The first time you are thirsty you will walk around the building looking for a water cooler. It will not be there. No good telling anyone that water coolers are not for water alone: they are social centers, information exchanges, and boosters of morale.

The British do not drink water.

There are two ways to get a drink:

A man who pours out a cup of tea is not to be trusted.

1. Ask your secretary

The coward simply asks his secretary, leaving to a young girl a problem that has baffled many a strong man:

"You want *water*, Mr. Brash? Why, are you ill?"

"No, no. Just to drink."

"Well, yes, sir, of course. You—you want it—*iced*?" *(They all know about Americans and ice.)*

"No, just water."

"Well. I wonder what we could *put* it in."

2. The old teacup method

Others find it less embarrassing to fend for themselves.

Remember that in every British office old, abandoned teacups can be found behind typewriters, in desk drawers, out-boxes, on window sills, everywhere you look. Some of these will be dust-covered, tea-stained, and with a residue of hardened sugar in the bottom.

Take one of these. No one will mind. If it is dry, put

it in your pocket. If it is still wet, no matter. Carry it openly and pretend you are looking for the tea lady, who rolls her cart perpetually through the halls. Everyone will help you find her.

"She was just here a moment ago, Mr. Brash!"

"Never mind, I'll find her!"

"She went *that* way, Mr. Brash!"

"Thank you, thank you so much!"

You may have to buy at least one cup of tea on the way. Maintain your sense of purpose and go directly to the lavatory. If by now the cup is full of tea, and you do not wish to drink it, pour it out quietly into the wash bowl. Do not let anyone see you. A man who pours out a cup of tea is not to be trusted.

Rinse the cup quickly, and fill it with cool water from the tap. It will be quite safe to drink. If others are there (and they may be; in the absence of water coolers, lavatories often became sexually segregated social centers) pretend to pop something into your mouth before drinking:

"Oh, headache, Mr. Brash?"

"Yes, frightful."

"Try one of mine." *(The British are always generous and helpful, and just as well supplied with pills as Americans.)*

"Thanks awfully. Have to take this bloody prescription. ("Bloody" is good here, especially, in the washroom.)*

You will succeed not only in getting a drink of water, but also in creating sympathy and understanding everywhere:

"Pity about old Brash. Obviously going through hell."

"Poor devil. No wonder he has to rush home early so often."

"Seems to have a *thirsty* look to me. Don't suppose he gets enough tea, eh?"

After a short while you, too, will become addicted to tea, and will wonder why in the world anyone wants to drink a glass of water. There is nothing, you will say, like a nice hot cup of tea, strong and dark, like American coffee. With milk, of course.

WHAT TO CALL PEOPLE IN THE OFFICE

Ever since you first became a junior executive, in America, you called everyone, including the Chairman of the Board, "Bill", or "Al", or "Tom".

In England you don't call *anyone* "Bill", or "Al", or "Tom", not even your brother. You call him "William", or "Albert", or "Thomas".

In the office, if he is a director you will not call him "William" unless you are a director, too, and not always even *then*. He may call you by your surname, as in: "Good morning, Brash!" as though you were the butler. You will call him, "Mr. Smith", and if he is Chairman of the Board you will call him, "Mr. Chairman".

What you call your secretary may be determined more by the nature of the business than by *her* nature. Only in American-oriented businesses, like publicity, will you call her "Ann", or "Mary", otherwise always, "Miss Mainwaring". She will always call you "Mr. Brash".

HOW TO TELL DIRECTORS FROM PEOPLE

Let us say you came to England as a Vice-President, the American equivalent of a junior knight in armor. You reached this position by qualities of dynamic leadership. (Other, lesser men got it only to persuade a client he was getting bigger thinking for his problems, or at least that his problems were bigger than he thought.)

In the States, as a Vice-President, you were monarch of practically all you surveyed.

In England it will not be quite the same.

"Miss Mainwaring, why is it that Brown-Winthrop, next door, gets the nice blue teacups and a plate of sweet biscuits every day—*free*—and I have to pay threepence for a chipped white cup of tea?"

"Well, Mr. Brash, Mr. Brown-Winthrop *is* a Director, you know."

"And his tea tastes better, too!"

"Yes, sir, he has the Directors' tea."

"But I'm a Vice-President!"

"I'd been meaning to ask you, sir. What *is* a Vice-President?"

No one will know what a Vice-President is, especially since your English company has no president, only a Managing Director.

You may, in an emergency, seek the nearest oasis:

"Sorry, Mr. Brash, you can't get in there without a key. That's the *Directors'* lavatory, sir."

"But I'm a Vice-President!"

"It's just a short walk down the hall, sir."

You will, on occasion, even be expected to stand when a Director comes into a room, as though he were a lady. You will feel, at this stage, that Directors are arrogant bullies, totally ignorant of Industrial Democracy.

When an American Vice-President has a brilliant idea, people rise up on all sides and argue with him.

Some of them will even tell him it is stupid, and this may be enough to stop him from going ahead with it, for hours.

In England when a company does something really stupid, you can be sure that an arrogant Director thought of it, that the people around him were horrified—and meekly said, "Yes, Sir!"

Try at first to bring them the blessings of American-style Industrial Democracy. Show them how a large company can be run entirely by meetings, with no one really in charge, and no one knowing which way it is going.

In England a Director will be in charge, though he is usually out of the office, and no one can find him, or dares to ask him where he was when they do.

You will soon find an easy way to deal with all this.

GET DOWN ON THEIR LEVEL

Next time a visiting Captain of your Industry comes to London from New York, have an earnest talk with him:

"Uh, how's it going, Brash?"

"Brash, sir. Very well indeed. I *like* these people. Matter of fact, sir, I'd like to get *right down there with them*, down on their level!"

"I like that, Bash, I like that! Down on their level, eh?"

"Yes, sir. Pull off my stripes, if you like— temporarily, that is—and let me get in there with the *men*. It's the American thing to do!"

This is bound to win you friends in high places:

"Good boy, that Bash! No gold braid about that lad! Just wants to be a Director, like the other guys.

Think we should give him a bit more money, just to make it even."

In no time you will have the blue teacups, a key to the posh lavatory, new office furniture, and a company car. It will seem to you, on the surface, that you are doing well.

Responsibility will be thrust upon you. Accept it— and select the proper persons to do the actual work.

One important area, however, you may want to enter yourself.

HOW TO HANDLE YOUR ADVERTISING AGENCY

Everyone knows that advertising is the life blood of industry. This is true in England, also, and if you are to get rich, you will have to learn how to get the most out of your advertising agency. It will need your help and guidance. Give them freely.

First, however, you will have to learn a few of the basic differences between British and American advertising.

It is different from America

You will remember your New York agency as a place of frenzy, where everyone screamed, gibbered, and trembled. Your slightest suggestion set off hysterical orgies of work:

"Well, boys, we'll all meet Mr. Brash again tomorrow, huh? George, you and Freddie and Mabel finish the rough copy on your nine sets of ads by seven tonight, the artists can do some roughs overnight, and we'll get the stats and some dummy photos in by ten in the morning, do up a few finals by noon, and meet Mr. Brash at two-thirty, right?"

Your function was to calm their nerves, to steer a wise and simple course through a hundred different versions, to keep your committees, their committees, and the various joint committees from making a complete hash of the whole business.

In London, the problem will be different.

In England, advertising is a lower caste

In America, where money is everything, advertising men are in a very high *caste* because they make money so quickly. The man who handled *your* advertising was probably the richest man you knew, with a great estate, a big yacht, and seven cars. He was as high in *caste* as a Duke, or Dee-yook, in England.

This is not true in London, where advertising men are in the same *caste* as piano tuners, sign painters, and press agents. Though they are not untouchable, they are not always asked to the nicest parties.

This is especially true of the men who do the thinking. They are kept downstairs in small cells, drink tea out of chipped cups, are not allowed to see the light of day, and are rarely permitted to speak to clients.

Everyone will be worried about finding new people to do the work. They will ask you:

"Mr. Brash, how do American agencies *recruit* people?"

"Once a week they open the door for ten minutes and take the names of the first two hundred applicants."

"You mean—people over there want to work for advertising agencies?"

"Doesn't *everyone*?"

How to get anything done

In London you will find little gibbering frenzy. Let us say you have had a long meeting, and have stated your need for new work:

"That's very clear, Mr. Brash. I should suggest that our people meet internally on this, very soon. Would Thursday week be all right? We could discuss preliminary notions. Perhaps a fortnight after that we could discuss rough ideas with Mr. Brash."

Your first impulse will be to bang on the table, or shout loudly. This will simply cause embarrassment, and will not win you friends, or get the work done more quickly.

Do not make difficult demands. Encourage them. With Americans, British admen often have inferiority complexes, and these can inhibit the creative processes:

"I think that's very good!"

"You really like it, Mr. Brash?"

"Don't often get this quality, even in New York!"

(This will sometimes be true, too.)

You will find that your clear-headed guidance will make all the difference. (You were clear-headed in New York, too—it was the other nineteen guys on the committee who were mixed up.)

While the British are doing two or three versions, the American committees will be tearing up fifteen or twenty, so that in the end they will come out about even, and the final results will be very much the same.

Look around you

Little by little, the child-like quality of British advertising is disappearing. ("Guinness is *Good* for you!" "Bovril Puts Beef Into You!").

Inspirations, proved and tested, are moving in across the Atlantic every day, to bring Britain up to advertising maturity. Already the blessings of hard sell, bad breath, body smells, and washing demonstrations are here—and the fascinating animated diagrams of stomach linings, diseased livers, and constipated intestines are on the way. Every American knows how much the future holds in store.

Britain is getting right into step and before you know it you will feel completely at home. You will have to stop and think whether you are in Piccadilly Circus or Times Square.

LABOR LEADERS CAN WORK FOR YOU

Do not actually come to grips with British Labor. It is a pitfall into which Americans can easily drop. Few have survived.

You will never understand British labor leaders because they seem more interested in striking a blow in the class war than they do in raising the hourly wage rate. The American labor leaders you know care nothing about the class war; they know they have already won it.

Let labor troubles work for you. You will find they can be a real boon, especially if there are rivals who need to be temporarily immobilized:

"Well, Bash, I guess you gotta get in there on this strike thing."

"Be glad to supervise it, sir, but for the day-to-day dealings, people like you and me are basically too *generous*. We need somebody like Sir Keith, with a man-on-horseback approach."

As the talks go on, month after month, be generous with your encouragement:

"Certainly do admire your fortitude, Keith. Good show!"

Once it is certain the company will have to do *something*, use a well-tried British device: suggest a committee, or commission, to investigate the whole issue.

Nothing can happen until the commission reports, in several years, by which time the whole situation will have changed completely, the directors will have changed jobs, and the labor leaders will have been elected to Parliament. It will be time to start the whole process over again.

RISE TO THE TOP

It will not matter what you *do* as a director—as long as you are careful never to look foolish.

After a decent interval, you will be ready for the next visit of your Captain of Industry:

"Well, say, you're gettin' to look like a real limey, Bash!"

"Brash, sir. Had a wonderful effect, your idea of putting me down on their level. Nothing like the old shirt sleeves!"

(This will be a figure of speech. You will never see any actual shirt sleeves, above the cuffs, in your whole British business career.)

"I like that, Bash! Less chiefs and more Indians, I say!"

"Might make more room at the old work bench, sir, if you'd just move me into Sir Keith's old room."

"What funny little name did they have for him, Bash?"

"Something-Director, I think."

"What won't they think of next?"

"I don't require being a Vice-President, sir, or anything flashy like that. Just another working stiff."

BE DEMOCRATIC

Once you are the Managing Director, you will realize you were completely wrong about arrogant directors. They are quite democratic, and in fact will do anything you tell them. Meetings will be a joy to you, and will take only a fraction of the time the old American discussion meetings did.

Try to be as democratic as possible with everyone. Always remember to let them sit down again, and try to listen, briefly, to their sides of the question:

"I must apologize for interrupting, Brown-Winthrop."

"I *quite* understand, Mr. Brash."

"Do write it out for me, like a good fellow."

Remember that a workable idea can come from anyone, no matter how humble his position, though it may often need to be properly shaped and presented.

The extra girl will be helpful, the Bentley will be useful in getting about London quickly, and having a driver is the *only* real solution to the parking problem.

You will feel by now that your position is impregnable—though you will discover later that this is not quite the case.

"ARE MANAGING DIRECTORS RICH?"

The answer is, no, they are not.

You may think you are *going* to be rich until you talk

"Remember, a workable idea can come from anyone."

to your British tax man. You may find that, somehow, you have less money left over than you did before.

But there *is* a way to get rich, as we shall discover in good time.

At this moment, however, you will feel expansive. You will believe—too soon!—that you are ready to take your place in the aristocracy.

15

The Dream House and How to Rebuild It

EVEN before you know you are going to be the Managing Director, your wife will *sense* it, no one knows how.

"Oh, Buckley, I'm so glad we can afford it now, because——"

"Afford what, Peg?"

"Don't let's talk about money,"

"I *wasn't*."

"I saw the most gorgeous Manor House in the whole world!" *(You will think you have heard this line before.)* "And we can just *steal* it far seventeen."

"I thought you said fifteen."

"Not that one, it's been Done Over now. You couldn't touch it for twenty-five."

"Twenty-five thousand pounds! That's seventy thousand dollars!"

"The cheap way is to do it over yourself."

Write this phrase, "the cheap way is to do it over yourself" on a piece of paper and press it in a heavy book, like a flower. Take it out later and look at it, when you are older, and wiser.

Meanwhile your mission is two-fold, and doubly dangerous. You will be trapped midway between a horde of British estate agents, skilled and ruthless and operating on their home ground—and on the other side a woman driven mad with desire, surrounded by houses which seem to be breathtakingly stately and at prices which she thinks are ridiculous.

AUCTIONS AND HOW TO USE THEM

Play for time. Your best ally is the popular British custom of house auctions.

Let us say your wife has another uncontrollable urge to buy a house:

"Oh, Buckley, just listen to this ad! Two acres, stables, a ballroom, and——"

"Can't possibly touch *this* one, Peg! And it's up for auction. We might steal it for *nothing*!"

No woman can resist a house auction, with its heady grab-bag atmosphere. Take her to as many as you can. They will be free, and full of local color.

"Wasn't that your bid, Buckley?"

"Me? No, I was just scratching my nose!"

"He just said, 'Sold!'. It went for thirteen thousand!"

"They're welcome to it at *that* price, don't you think?"

You will be able to spend pleasant months, and even years, learning about the countryside, and sharpening your sense of values.

CHOOSE YOUR OWN TIME

Keep this going just long enough—but not too long. A wife driven too far may jump up at auctions and make bids you will both regret.

Choose your moment before it is too late. There is nothing like a house in hand to keep your wife out of the market.

"Think I've got it at last, Peg. Lovely house up for auction."

"Oh, not another auction, Buckley!"

(This is a good sign. It indicates she is becoming more manageable.)

"This one is different. Auction's in a month, but it says they may sell by private agreement ahead of auction."

"Let's talk to them, then."

"I have. Think we can steal it at twelve. Under thirty-four thousand bucks!"

Be sure you have chosen one that is full of furniture, and with a presentable garden. You will be able to show it to your wife with confidence:

"My it *is* beautiful, Buckley!"

"You understand it doesn't actually *include* the furniture, Peg."

"Wasn't that your bid—?"

"Of course not. Just look around, though. What lovely chandeliers!"

"Beautiful bookshelves."

"And what a nice kitchen! A few buckets of paint and a roller and we can move right in!"

Make a ten per cent down payment to seal the bargain, and they will call off the house auction. There will still be a furniture auction, though. It will be called, "Contents of the Residence". Go to it. You will have fun watching people buy up the old knick-knacks, and trying to pick up real bargains:

"Haven't I seen those men somewhere before, Peg?"

"They're dealers. They come to all the auctions. Quiet, now, they're going to bid on that cute little table."

"I'll go as high as eight pounds on it, Peg."

"He just started at seventy-five."

"That's over two hundred bucks!"

"It says they're going to auction the chandeliers!"

"They can't do that! That's ours!"

The day after the auction will be *your* day. The hurly-burly will be over, the furniture and all the knick-knacks will be removed—and anything that is left will be yours:

"Oh, Buckley, I could cry! Those lovely chandeliers, all ripped out!"

"Just a jagged hole, and two twisted wires!"

"Even the wall fixtures! *Everything*, all torn out!"

"Look at the walls, all full of holes——"

"They've even ripped out the book cases!"

"Look at the floors, where the carpet used to be—they're not even finished. It looks like a stable."

Every fitted carpet, stair carpet, curtain, and fixture of any kind will be torn out. On the first day it will be best not to go into the kitchen.

"Oh, Buckley, they've ripped out the stove, and the ice box—and there's only this stone basin and wooden drain-board!"

"Well, the walls seem to be standing, anyway, Peg."

ONLY THE WOOD WILL HAVE TO GO

In most cases the walls *will* be standing. They are usually heavy masonry, built to last for centuries. Only the wooden parts will have to be replaced.

"Buckley, I had the most wonderful talk with Mrs Frampton, next door. She's *very* nice. She thinks we're really *brave* to buy this house, after looking in the roof."

"*Did* we look in the roof?"

"*I* didn't—did you? She says it's full of those beetles."

"Is that all? I'm going up there right now, with some Flit."

"Do you think it's safe?"

Take a flashlight and go up into the roof timbers. The beetles will not hurt you.

"See, Peg, not a beetle in sight."

"Not a one. Mrs Frampton suggested you stick a pocket knife into one of the beams."

"What do you know! Goes right through, doesn't it? All full of sawdust. I think they're *all* like this."

"What do you suppose is holding up the roof, Buckley?"

"Let's get out of here!"

A man from the woodworm industry, one of the most thriving in Britain, will come out to see you. He will not seem especially alarmed:

"Oh, no, Mr. Brash, it's quite safe. Roof shouldn't collapse for a number of years. Simply the House Longhorn Beetle, *Hylotrupes bajulus*."

"Then where are they?"

"Never see the beetles. Just the larvae, inside the beams. Little devils stay in there for years, eating away! Every house in Surrey's got 'em, but you've got more than your share, Mr. Brash. Just a matter of replacing about half the roof timbers and spraying the rest. It's downstairs I'm really worried about."

"Beetles down there, too?"

"Oh, no, sir. Just the little fellows, who made all those pin holes in the floors and door frames. Common furniture beetle."

"The floor and door frames will have to go, too?"

"May save quite a few of them, sir. That is, the ones that don't have dry rot, too. We handle rot, too, sir. One of our specialties."

Usually the whole thing can be fixed up for three or four thousand dollars, and in a matter of a few short months.

NOW FOR THE HEATING!

However, there is no need to wait for the woodworm man. While they are spraying and sawing the roof and door frames, you can be showing the British how to heat a house.

Let us assume you bought the house partly because you saw radiators in the living room. Do not count too heavily on these:

"Buckley, the heating man says it would be simpler just to pull out the old radiators in the living room, and start over."

"Why?"

"He has to put in small bore heating—that's with the little pipes and a water pump—unless we want to tear down all the walls and ceilings."

"We can keep the old furnace, then?"

"Well, it seems our old burner has a kind of wick, like an oil lamp. It isn't a blower like the ones at home. The man says it will handle four or five more radiators——"

"We need twenty more!"

Just buy the kind of oil burner the British make for factories. For another three or four thousand dollars they will put in the whole system, with thermostats, electric clock control, and everything.

"The oil burner man brought up one little thing, Buckley. Electricity."

"We do have electricity—don't we?"

"But it isn't turned on, and before the Electricity Board will do that, they have to inspect the wiring."

ELECTRICITY CAN BE SIMPLE

Since electricity is nationalized, you will find that the man who inspects your wiring can also contract to put it right, if it isn't right. This creates interesting situations:

"Then I just have to rewire the first floor?"

"Yes, sir."

"Then the ground floor is all right."

"Unless you want to put in the new ring-wiring system, sir."

"For an extra two hundred pounds. You said that wasn't legally necessary.'

"No, sir."

"Then it's perfectly safe to keep the ground floor wiring?"

"I didn't say *that*, sir."

"You wouldn't condemn it."

"No, sir."

"Then we're all set if you do the first floor."

"For the lighting circuit, sir. Now we come to the power circuit."

"There are two *different* circuits?"

"Oh, yes, sir."

"And different plugs?"

"Yes, sir."

"Couldn't we put them all on the *same* circuit?"

"Wouldn't be safe to do *that*, sir. Not with 240 volts."

HOW TO COUNTER-SHOCK

If you feel vexed beyond endurance, try counter-shock tactics:

"Actually, we were thinking of just *doing away with it*."

"With what, sir?"

"Electricity. Gas light, you know. Coming thing in America." *(This is a line that always strikes terror into British hearts: "It's a coming thing in America". They turn pale and tremble, as though a shiny, lunatic monster were moving inexorably to engulf them.)*

"Is it really, sir?"

"Bound to catch on here."

"Let's examine these plans again, sir."

NOW WHAT ABOUT PLUMBING?

Many Americans pull up the floors four times, once for the woodworm man, once for the central heating, once for the electricity, and once for plumbing. No laws require this, but it is rarely possible to schedule the various and unrelated teams at the same time.

Try to get someone to look at the pipes while someone else has the floors up:

"You *are* fortunate, sir. Most of your pipes are *inside* the walls."

"Good. No winter freeze-ups for us."

"Only the drains, sir. They're outside."

"You mean we can get the water *into* the bowls. We just won't be able to get it out?"

You will probably have to replace only the bowls, baths, and toilets, and put in a shower bath. Your main problem will be to get them all started.

MOVE RIGHT IN WITH THEM

At first you will think you are lucky not to be living in the house while all this is going on.

However, you may be startled to discover that for the first few months, nothing *is* going on. The contracts are all signed, everything is ready to go, and nothing happens.

You will drive up to the house every day and look in. No one will be there. Nothing will have changed, except that the garden is getting wilder and wilder.

But one day you will discover action:

"Oh, Buckley, look! There's a truck in the drive!"

"Good! It's starting. They're really doing something, too! Hear that roaring noise? Sounds like blowtorches!"

You will rush in to welcome the workmen, excited to find out what is being done first:

"Not here, Peg. Sounds like it's coming from the laundry."

The sound will grow louder and louder. You will rush into the laundry and find a group of men gathered tensely around a structure of bricks, on the tile floor. One will be holding a blow torch, and another will be steadying a kettle.

"Why, Buckley, they're making *tea*!"

MAKE TEA AND SEE

You will discover that very little real work will be done until you are on hand to *make the tea for them*. Move in as soon as possible, on a camping basis. It is better if you have electricity, or gas, for cooking, but if not there are many good alcohol or kerosene stoves on the market.

"Well, how'd we do today, Peg?"

"I kept count, Buckley. We only had the woodworm, heating, and electricity men today, and I made exactly fifty-seven cups of tea. Tomorrow, when the plumbers get here, too, we're going to set a new record."

Make the tea good and strong. It is a real stimulant, and the time the men take drinking it in mid-morning ("elevenses") and mid-afternoon ("tea") is often made up for by increased concentration, vigor, and strength of purpose. The considerate housewife furnishes tea to go with their lunches, too, and many believe that a few shillings worth of sweet biscuits (cookies to you) served with tea and elevenses are good investments, increasing good will and adding quick energy.

Of course there are days when elevenses, lunch, and

Make the tea good and strong.

tea seem to blend into one long tea ceremony; on these days the extra concentration and vigor are enormous, but do not appear to be used in your behalf.

After three or four months of this the mechanical work will be done, and you will be ready for the men who will plaster up the holes in the walls, and the one who will refinish (and in some cases rebuild) the floors.

WHERE TO KEEP YOUR CLOTHES

One day you will feel that everything is truly ready, and you have a real house of your own. At this time a number of new problems may begin to raise their heads:

"Buckley, I just happened to think. There aren't any closets. Where are we going to hang our clothes?"

No matter how much furniture you brought from

the States, you will not have wardrobes, the large box-like objects in which all Europeans hang their suits and dresses. And you will resist buying new ones, at about £50 or $140 apiece, since you will not want to take them back with you.

Do not despair. Wardrobes of all shapes, sizes, and colors are sold every day at furniture auctions in England. Find them!

"Come outside and see it, Buckley. Isn't it wonderful!"

"What is it?"

"A wardrobe, for hanging clothes. Twelve feet wide, not counting the bulge, and I got it for just nine pounds!"

"Striking shade of blue, Peg."

"You can paint it, Buckley."

"I was just thinking—how are we going to get it up the stairs?"

A word of caution: Wardrobes are like boats, built in basements. Curb your enthusiasm until you measure the stairway, your bedroom doors, and the wardrobe. It is cheaper to by a *new*, compact wardrobe than to remove your outside walls.

TURN ON THE HEAT!

From the day you arrive in England you will long for one moment: when you are master of your own heating system, and can turn it on.

Cold evenings in late September, once so uncomfortable, will be warm and cozy. Now at last, you will say, with real American central heating, you have the best of both worlds.

This will be true up to a point—the point at which it begins to get really cold:

"Buckley, I'm frozen! Is the heat on?"

"Radiators all hot as a pistol, Peg. Have been for hours."

"Why isn't it getting any warmer in here?"

You will discover you are burning about £35, or $100 worth of oil every month, and having trouble keeping the temperature above sixty.

"I was just wandering around in the roof space, Peg. Do you realize there's nothing between us and the cold, cold world except about half an inch of plaster on the ceilings? No insulation at all!"

You will begin to notice, too, that the British have different ideas of floor-covering than you have:

"Buckley, I could hardly help laughing at all the stuff the Framptons had on their floors. They had fitted carpets, and rugs on top of them. Certainly doesn't take the place of pretty scatter rugs and pretty, polished floors!"

"Would you like to try feeling our pretty, polished floor, Peg?"

You will discover you can almost freeze water on the bare, polished floor of your living room, no matter how much heat you have in the radiators. Few British homes have basements, and there is often nothing under the floor boards but a cold, winter wind, whistling up through the cracks. This is why they use a thick felt underlay, then a fitted carpet, and often rugs on top of that.

"Will you close the window, Buckley?"

"It *is* closed, Peg."

"Then why are the drapes blowing like flags?"

Many Americans find that their gaily printed cotton "drapes" (a term which has no meaning in England) give little protection against the winds that whistle past the window frames. After a while you will change to British style curtains, as heavy as overcoats, lined and quilted, and like the British, you will draw them snugly as soon as the sun goes down.

Once you insulate the attic, and learn some of the carpet and curtain tricks of the natives, you will be just as warm with your central heating as they are without it. Indeed, sometimes warmer.

"SHOULD WE BUY ANCESTORS?"

Some Manor Houses do come complete with a set of ancestors on the walk, and have indeed been bought by Americans *for that reason alone.*

Other Americans bring their ancestors with them. American ancestors, however, tend to look stern and puritanical, making not only poor wall coverings, but poor companions. They will often be photographs, perhaps Daguerrotypes or sepiatones, or otherwise monochromatic.

British ancestors, on the other hand, can be colorful and sizeable, and though often haughty, are seldom puritanical. You may ask: "Can we buy some?" The answer is, yes, you can. The English have far more ancestors than they need, and will be glad to sell you all you want. You will find them in any auction room, often cheaper by the square foot than a good wallpaper, more durable, and better for covering awkward pipes, and holes in plaster.

"That's a pretty good one, Peg. Nice size for that place where the gas pipe broke through."

"I'm not sure, Buckley. It seems to me he wouldn't *go* with the others, and you've got to have a matching set."

Polyglot, unmatched ancestors give a patchy, untended appearance, like an unmowed lawn. The entire group must seem to be going *in the same general direction*. On the other hand, it is no good to try to match them too closely. An occasional vacant stare or look of confusion shows a resolve not to hide skeletons in the closet.

Try to avoid ancestors with a strong look of disapproval. Weeks of down–the–nose staring by a well-medalled adopted great-grandfather can sap your self-confidence.

If you cannot find suitable ancestors, or not enough to cover all the holes and pipes, there will be unlimited quantities of misty landscapes in both oil and water colors, equally sturdy and even lower in price.

Try to avoid ancestors with a strong look of disapproval.

BE A LAND OWNER!

Almost before you know it, your house will pop into shape. You will be able to sit back and know that you are, in a sense, the Lord of your own Manor. A little corner of England is yours—or *almost* yours.

Some Americans discover, a bit too late, little tricks of British real estate that were never properly explained to them. Your neighbor will be glad to set you right:

"Oh, uh, Mr. Frampton—I got this letter in the mail, I mean post. It's a bill for *ground rent*."

"Yes, that's right."

"*Rent*? I bought this house! I own it!"

"You own the *house*, Mr. Brash, but somebody else owns the land it's on. You have a leasehold. I believe the lease is up in about nineteen years."

"Then I don't own the house any more?"

"Actually, it's worse than that. If the owner of the land demands it, you'll have to tear the house down, at your own expense!"

Remember the word "leasehold". Remember the word "freehold", too, which means you do own the land.

In fact, it is a good idea to write these words down, several times.

MAKE IT A BEAUTY SPOT!

Pleasant and satisfying as you will find the rebuilding of your dream house, you will find it is even more rewarding—though more difficult too, at times!—to give it a worthy setting.

We shall move quickly, then, to blossoms and greenery, to the leafy world of growing things.

16

How to Beat the Back Yard

EVERYTHING GROWS IN ENGLAND

EVEN before the last workman has left, you will discover you are living in the middle of a jungle. Things grow no faster on the banks of the Amazon than they do on this damp and fertile island.

In a few weeks your grass will be knee-high, the weeds will be matted undergrowth, and the shrubbery will look like a rain forest. It will become a matter of local concern, even of crisis:

"Mrs. Frampton was saying this morning, Buckley, that this place used to have a full-time gardener. They used to pay him a pound a day."

"Where is he now?"

"We're all trying to locate him—but they say he *is* over seventy-five, and——"

You will discover that all the landed gentry still have dreams of cheap and faithful retainers. They will be everywhere, like wood fairies and leprechauns, and just as hard to put your hands on.

You may even try to recruit a gardener yourself. Let us say you discover, on a neighboring plot, a manure-covered wretch in an old sweater, his trousers stuffed into mud-caked rubber boots. He will be stumbling from dunghill to greenhouse to potting shed. You will assume your gardening problems are over:

"I say, my man, is your master about?"

"Ow, no, guv'nor."

"I just wanted to ask him if it would be all right to speak to you about doing some work in my yard, if you have time."

"Your *yard*, guv'nor?"

"Yes."

"The yard shouldn't take a minute, guv'nor. It's the garden that takes the time. Blimey, it's all I can do to handle this 'un."

NEVER SAY "YARD"

You will have made your first mistake about gardens. To call a British garden a "back yard" is like calling an American's back yard a garbage dump.

The British "back yard" is an area, usually made of concrete, where he keeps things like garbage cans, which he calls dust bins.

The difference is much more than just a word. It is the difference between two worlds. You may not be impressed by the interior of British homes, but you will be overwhelmed by the magnificence of their gardens.

More Americans in England are broken by gardens than by any other cause. You will have to lick the garden, or the garden will lick you. Just "letting the garden go" will not work. You would become a social outcast and an object of public scorn.

"I give up, Peg. I even tried that manure-covered wretch two places down—the one in the old sweater and boots——"

"Yes, his wife, Lady Walloughby, was telling me. He is Sir Noël Walloughby, and he can't find a gardener, either."

"Oh, no!"

"I think it's just that no one is willing to pay enough for them, Buckley."

"Peg, with the six and a half per cent we're paying on the mortgage, the ground-rent, the bills for the heating, plumbing, woodworm, and electricity contractors, plus all the school fees—I may have to go out evenings and work in *other* people's gardens! We're heading for bankruptcy!"

HELP YOUR NEIGHBORS

Do not dwell on your own problems. Help your neighbors. And you can, more than you know.

Remember that Americans have been through all this before. You come from a country where gardeners are called "landscape architects", drive Chrysler station wagons, and make more money than British Managing Directors.

You have known all your life you could never *dream* of having a gardener. The British gentleman really knows this, too, but he doesn't *believe* it yet. When his house was built and his gardens laid out, his family lived in a world of cap-touching gardeners who would grovel for a few coppers. They have now all disappeared, leaving him marooned in a wilderness of the world's most elaborate gardens, without a hand to help him but his own.

He has dozens of flower beds, greenhouses, starting frames, and potting sheds. No sooner does a petal fall than the plant is snatched quivering from the earth, and replaced by something in the greenhouse, ready to burst instantly into flower. Every moment, all weekend, he rushes from herbaceous border to compost heap with seedlings, bulbs, and cuttings by the thousand, hacking, forking, weeding, transplanting, spraying, and mowing.

The result is breath-taking—and he never has time to sit down and look at it.

You will think at first that your neighbor is a lover of nature:

"Must be wonderful to love growing things, Mr. Frampton!"

"*Love* 'em? Are you mad, Mr. Brash? Hate the bloody things! Hate gardening! Don't you?"

"Why spend all your time doing it?"

"There's another way?"

Feverish activity will be going on all around you. You will feel you are in the middle of an ant-hill. If you sit in the sun in a deck chair, you will be the only man for miles around who is, because (*a*) they have no deck chairs, only a few straight chairs, in which to snatch a cup of tea between cross-pollinations, and (*b*) if the sun is shining they will refuse to admit it.

Your object will be three-fold: to lift the yoke from their backs, to keep it from landing on yours, and to be loved and respected by everyone.

There are a number of well-tried methods:

1. Appreciate

You will be in a unique position. With everyone else working all the time, there will be no one else around to look at all the gardens they are working on. An ounce of appreciation is worth a pound of work:

"Oh, I say, Mr. Frampton, that border is absolutely smashing!"

"Awf'ly good of you to say that, Mr. Brash." *(He will be lying on his belly in a mixture of compost and rainwater, weeding the michaelmas daisies.)*

"Never saw hollyhocks look so pretty!" *(Don't admit the knowledge of more than five or six names of flowers.)*

"May be because they're lupins, old boy."

"Wonderful what you fellows know about flowers! Wish you could pop over to my place sometime and give me a start an mine."

"Love to. Let's have a go. Any time." *(He will mean it, too, but you know, and he really knows in his heart, that he won't have a minute until the snow flies.)*

You will be welcome everywhere, and you will be cementing lasting friendships:

"This fellow Brash. Not the typical American at all. Really fine sense of appreciation of gardens."

"Have you seen *his*?"

"My fault, really. Been meaning to get over there and give him a start."

2. Ask for advice

Any one of your neighbors, picked at random, will know more about flowers than Luther Burbank. Ask freely for information. It will be easy to see which blossoms are closest to his heart. Select his biggest, most luxuriant growth and approach it with a whoop:

"No wonder you're famous for your peonies, Nigel!" *(By this time you will be firm friends.)*

"That's a dahlia, Buckley."

"Could I have a cutting for my place?"

"Many as you like, lad, but the roots would work better. Look like potatoes. I'll save you some."

Choose a time when he is a gibbering animal.

Once your neighbors begin to regard you as a little lost boy, you will be able to relax and enjoy the flowers on all sides.

"Seems to me Brash just *sits* all weekend."

"Poor lad. Waiting for a cutting of my hydrangeas. Good spirit, though, for a Yank."

3. Emancipate them

Remember that your real mission is to set them free. It is far easier than you think.

Choose a time when your neighbor is on the point of physical exhaustion, a gibbering animal, dripping with sweat, stung with nettles, and bleeding from thorns; in short, the typical British country gentleman on a late Sunday afternoon.

Destroy his will to fight with a long, cool drink. Settle him in a luxurious deck chair, and keep the women away. (He will have an uncontrollable urge to bound up and down every time one looms on the horizon.) Then begin to undermine his character. The British character takes a lot of undermining, but it can be done.

"Can't help admiring the way you keep everlastingly at it, Nige. Shows real character."

"Nonsense, Buckley. Lot of silly asses. Bloody waste of time."

(It is impossible to top the British in criticizing themselves, and there is no use trying.)

"Now you take the slip-shod American method of automatic gardening——"

"Automatic?" *(There will be a faint gleam of hope in his nearly lifeless eyes.)*

"Lazy bastards. No central flower beds. No annuals. No transplanting. Just a lawn and a ride-able lawn mower. Shrubs all around.* Prune 'em once a year. Just loll around all weekend. Another drink, Nige?"

"Just loll around, eh?" *(His hand will be shaking.)*

"The Americans can sure learn a lesson from you boys, Nige."

A word of caution: It is always wise to be careful whom you set free. If your windows actually *overlook* your neighbor's garden, emancipate other, more distant friends, and allow your neighbor to blunder on as he was. It will improve his character. Keep your shrubbery on his side low. There is nothing like a backdrop of flowers to set off a pretty lawn.

---

* Rhododendrons, hydrangeas, and azaleas all grow like weeds in England. Just stand back and keep out of their way.

4. Be exotic

If you are adventurous, try the exotic approach. Obtain seeds, or shoots, of obscure perennials, so hardy they will choke out anything:

"Great Scott, Buckley, what is *that*?"

"Lumbricus oviparus tendentious, actually. *(Any names ending in "us" will do.)* Don't know the common name. Grows like a weed in Guatamala." *(Choose any country outside the Commonwealth. He will know nothing about it. The plant grows like a weed in England, too, but no need to mention that.)*

"Fascinating. May I have a cutting?"

"All you want, Nige. Do remember, though, that it must be planted an hour before dawn."

"Before dawn, eh?"

"Not too much trouble, really, if you *love* 'em. The long nights go like a shot."

"*What* long nights, Buckley?"

"During germination, Nige. Only a few short weeks. One slip then and—bang! you've got fellacosis! Not the thing for the daytime gardener!"

Though this course is risky, the returns can be rich indeed. You can have long, lazy days in the sun, and be building character, too:

"Just look, Nigel! There's Brash again, prone on his bloody patio!"

"Don't be too harsh with him, old boy. Been up the last three nights with his *lumbricus*!"

5. Use a clipper

An electric hedge clipper will pay handsome dividends. (NOTE: Use rubber gloves and a three-pin plug if you have standard 240-volt current, or you will soon be dead.) With a clipper, almost any patch of weeds or matted undergrowth, if densely grown, can be clipped into a neat and decorative pattern in a matter of moments.

"God, Buckley, what is that?"

"*Ulricus commonatus majorcus.* Interesting, isn't it?"

"Always shaped like that?"

"Traditional way of cutting it, Nige. Fertility symbol."

"Wants a lot of fertilizer?"

"Only its own clippings. Always *leave them where they fall.* Mixed with a pinch of salt in early spring."

Some American experts have found that the rotary type of lawn mower, usually called a roto-scythe in England, can be equally useful. Unlike the traditional cylindrical type of mower, it can transform high growths of bracken, nettles, and other weeds into a lawn-like appearance, *no matter how long neglected.*

"Interesting, ah, lawn you have there, Buckley."

"Striving for *texture*, Nige. Once you get away from the old *velvetty* look, there's no limit to where you can go."

(Many, in fact, go to play golf, but you can go anywhere.)

6. Hire an Italian

No matter how skilful you become at garden management, there will be some heavy work that can be dangerous to the thinking man. For this purpose the British allow a number of Italian workmen to enter the country every year. You can usually hire them by the day, for six or seven dollars, or from about two to two and a half pounds.

There is no use trying to find them. Just hold still long enough and they will find you.

They work with enormous vigor, and fill the air with song. They have only two disadvantages: (1) they speak almost no English, and (2) they know nothing about English gardens.

Let us assume you will find a good one. Do not worry about his lack of skill. By this time you will have more than enough skill for both of you:

"Buckley, would you mind telling Luigi—no more cabbages in the formal garden?"

"I did."

"What did he say?"

"*Prego.*"

"He always says *prego.*"

"I'm sure he understood, Peg. Good man, Luigi. Green thumb. Grow anything."

You will have many happy surprises.

"*Talk* to him, Buckley. He's got the short flowers in the back, and the tall flowers in the front."

"We've been all through that, Peg. Got 'em all changed around."

"Mrs. Frampton says our herbaceous border is going to be lettuce in front, leeks in the middle, and rhubarb in back."

145

"AM I NOW LIVING LIKE A LORD?"

You may ask yourself, at this point, "Am I living like a Lord, at last?" And the answer is, yes, you are. You are living in a house that is slightly too large and too drafty, with a garden that is beyond your wildest efforts to manage, and with no idea how you are going to pay all your current bills.

You are living like the ordinary run-of-the-mill Lord.

You must move ahead rapidly, and before you know it you will be living like a Duke, or Dee-yook.

17

How to Live with the Upper Classes without Having Any Money

WHAT *ARE* THE UPPER CLASSES?

Do NOT fear being poor in England.

In America the upper classes are the people who have the money.

In England the upper classes are the people whose ancestors made money long ago—long enough so that everyone has forgotten how. It doesn't even matter very much whether they have it any more. Some of the Best People are as poor as they can be.

No one will mind if you have to be poor along with them.

You, too, can live the aristocratic life without spending any money. You will just have to learn a few simple, but lordly skills.

BE A SPORTSMAN

All the Best People in England are sportsmen. The sooner you can join them, the better.

Start with cricket. Once you have got cricket licked, the rest will be easy.

HOW TO PLAY CRICKET

You do not need to know how to play it, in person. A talking knowledge will be enough.

Go with your son to a cricket game. Any game, even one played by little boys, will be fine for a start. Throw yourself into it:

"Foul ball!"

"Shhhh, Father!"

"I was only whispering, Pete."

"This is *cricket*, Father!"

The first thing to remember is that cricket is QUIET. Unlike a baseball game, which can deafen you half a mile away, a cricket game cannot be heard at all, *even when you are there.*

Once a scandal was caused when the wives of some players were having a *conversation*, inside the clubhouse, during a match. The noise naturally "put everyone off."

"All I whispered, Pete, was that the batter ran on a foul ball."

"There *are* no foul balls, Father. The batsman can hit the ball behind him if he wishes."

"Run! Run!"

"Please, Father!"

"He hit it, why doesn't he run?"

"He doesn't have to run unless he is sure he will have time to get there."

"Then how do they put the guy out?"

"Sometimes it takes all day."

DO NOT RUSH IT

A complete game (called "match") can take *five full days*, from morning until evening, with breaks for lunch and tea.

The crowd maintains keen interest during the entire period. True, it will seem to you at first that no one is paying attenion, or even looking at the game. People will be reading newspapers, playing cards, eating, whispering among themselves about something else, and apparently sleeping—but if you spend several days with them, you too will learn to share their tension and excitement.

Do not make the common American mistake of suggesting ways to "speed up the game". Try a different wicket:

"Did you like it, Buckley?"

"Fascinating, Nige. Did seem to me that things were a bit *rushed*, though. Do you feel that five days are enough for a full game?"

It is not true that all British women hate cricket. Many merely dislike it. You will find some who can discuss it without emotion or rancor. However, if your dinner-table companion is female, try to talk of something else.

"IS FOOTBALL FOR THE UPPER CLASSES?"

First let us define our terms. The game most resembling American football is Rugby. The one called "football" is soccer.

Rugby, played at most of the fashionable Public Schools, was originally a game of the upper classes. Lower class critics claim, in fact, that it is being dropped continually on their heads for generations that gives the upper classes some of their special qualities.

"SHOULD I LET MY SON PLAY RUGBY?"

If you had any qualms about American football, Rugby will terrify you. It is American football without the armor, and almost without the whistle stops. No whistle blows when a knee touches the ground in Rugby. Players can be dragged and beaten over the whole field, and the game goes on. They tackle, pile up, and crash into each other at high speed dressed only in a jersey, shorts, and cleated boots. The timid wear a band of cloth around their heads to keep their ears from being torn off. They do not care if anything else is torn off.

FOOTBALL IS AN INDOOR SPORT

Do not make the mistake that soccer, or Association Football, is unspeakable among the upper classes, even though it is by far the most popular game among the masses. Football is played at Eton and other very private schools, and has many supporters among the best people.

Soccer is comparatively safe, even for the men on the field. But for every one of them there are tens of thousands of indoor players, marking the weekly printed forms of the football pools. If you predict enough scores you can win £100,000, or $280,000 for a bet of three pennies, tax free.

The pools are acceptable, even among the upper crust, partly because all Englishmen resist indoor activity. While marking his pools ticket he is indoors, but mentally outdoors, and thus can be indoors and outdoors at the same time.

TENNIS PLAYERS, STAY HOME

If you are a tennis addict, do not come to England— *unless you are sure you won't have to come back home.* England will spoil you forever.

In America tennis has a status midway between quoits and mah jong, and will continue to wane until the invention of the tennis cart, which will enable it to be played sitting down.

In England the upper classes—and almost everyone else—will join you playing tennis. Good clubs are everywhere, and your dues ("subscription") will be about 20% of what you would pay at an American club, if you could find one.

Try, if you can, to imagine a country that puts tennis on television five hours a day for two weeks, on two channels, as the British do during Wimbledon.

HOW TO PLAY DO-IT-YOURSELF GOLF

The British still play golf standing up. Golf carts have not yet penetrated even the upper classes.

Once you get used to walking again, you will be delighted. You may not at first believe the prices charged by most British golf clubs, which are sometimes less for a year than you have been paying for a month.

In fact, golf and tennis are so cheap, and driving, drinking, and smoking are so expensive that your health is sure to improve.

"CAN I BEAT THE HORSES?"

If you really want to wade in, elbow to elbow, with the very top people, find out where the horses are running.

They will all be there, any day of the week but Sunday. You will sometimes wonder what else they do.

Horse racing is the national sport of England. Race tracks are everywhere. As much space is given to horse racing on British sports pages as to all other sports combined.

As an old student of the Racing Form, you will assume you can beat the horses in England, and bolster up an inadequate income.

You will be profoundly shocked.

It is easy to bet at the track by "tote" or by bookie (they are legal), or at betting shops on every high street. It is easier to bet on a horse in England than it is to buy a cabbage.

It is much harder to win. The British know more about horses than Kentucky Colonels do. If you can win at British tracks, come back to America and you will be a rich man.

If you can keep from betting, horse racing in England can be a cheap pastime. At many tracks you can get in to certain sections (such as the "heath", the area in the middle) for nothing, and you can bet on the "tote" for as little as two shillings, or 28 cents.

On the other hand, if you want to splurge, you can spend more, without even betting, at a British track than you can anywhere. A box at Royal Ascot, with its own private dining room, maid, smoked salmon, strawberries, and all the clothes to go with it can cost thousands, for just four days.

HOW TO WIN AT CONVERSATION

But the basic British indoor sport is conversation, and it is played under rules that differ sharply from those of the American game. Without a little study and careful practice you will be quickly defeated, if not disgraced.

The educated English are skilled almost beyond belief, can talk knowingly about almost anything, and beautifully even about things of which they know nothing.

If you can play a good enough game at conversation, the British will not care a bit whether you have any money or not.

Do not be afraid to use the full force of your intellect. Once the British get used to your funny accent, they will understand almost everything you say. Though they leave school at an early age, their minds are quick, and they are eager to learn.

Beware of several dire pitfalls.

"SHOULD I BRAG?"

The answer is, no, you should not.

The British all live right on top of each other. They know that the man who never boasts is always one-up on the man who does—because everyone is sure to find out about it anyway.

You have an inherited tendency to brag, handed down from your frontier forefathers, who were continually driving their covered wagons into new and isolated areas. If they didn't brag, nobody would ever know.

Now is the time to change your ways.

The British will never openly criticize your boasting. They will delight in it.

Let us say you have been having Sunday noon cocktails at a neighbor's house. One member of the group has seemed to be absorbed by the saga of your famous six-minute mile at the fraternity intra-mural track meet. You will note a twinkle in his eye, and will take it for childlike admiration. Afterwards you may ask:

"What was that thin fellow's name again, Nige?"

"Oh, old Chawkins?"

"Pleasant chap. Seemed to be interested in running, but didn't have much to say, did he?"

"Not much he could add, Buckley. Won an Olympic gold medal in Rome, you know. Not something he'd be likely to bring up." *(He will give you a fleeting, sidelong glance that you will never forget, though you will often wish you could.)*

You will stop bragging as soon as you learn the British art of the *loaded understatement*:

"No, no, really! You mustn't exaggerate my influence in the White House. I've spent very little time there!" *(In fact, only on the guided tour, in 1956, but no need to be too specific.)*

Working in tandem, two or three Americans can often score heavily:

"Now you take Bud Round, for instance, Nige. Would he ever tell you he ambushed and machine-gunned a whole German platoon—single-handed? Not that boy!"

(Especially since he was in the quartermaster corps in Virginia during the whole war.)

You will be able to count on Bud to reciprocate:

"Buckley Brash? Bet he's never told you he shot down forty-six Zeroes, not counting twelve probables! Wild horses couldn't drag it out of him!"

Always deny these stories hotly:

"Is it true you shot down forty-six Zeroes, Mr. Brash?"

"Ridiculous! Frightfully inflated, all these reports. And how was anyone to know for sure?"

(Not you, certainly, as an Ensign in the accounts office.)

Soon you will have a reputation for well-documented modesty, so dear to British hearts.

LEAVE YOUR ESCUTCHEON AT THE DOOR

Do not bring your coat of arms with you, whether you have a dented one on a rusty shield, or the best new mail-order one that money can buy. You will avoid heart-ache.

Let us say, for example, you are equipped with expensive genealogical information and decide to use it to light up the drab little life of a British friend—one who lives, perhaps, in a seedy walk-up flat and drives an eight-year-old Morris Minor:

"Now you take my great-great-great grandfather, Derek. There was a real Briton! Got his coat of arms right here. We're practically sure he had a regular castle—moat and all!"

"You don't say, Brash. Fascinating."

You may be advised later:

"Ah, Buckley, I wouldn't stress that castle bit too much with Derek. Had his belly-full. Third son of Lord Thistledown, you know. Place the size of Waterloo Station."

"SHOULD WE FLOG?"

One day as you sit beside a kind and gentle English lady, she will smile sweetly across her cup of tea and ask:

"And how do *you* feel about flogging, Mr. Brash?"

You will think at first that she is joking, but she is not. The English are the kindest people on earth. And they are the only civilized people still alive who seriously discuss physical torture as a remedy for crime.

British schoolboys, as we have seen, are beaten with sticks. It is a status symbol. The higher the class of the school, the more likely the boys are to be beaten. You can tell a gentleman by the corrugations on his bottom, if you can get that close.

Some people believe this is another benefit of the affluent society that should be showered on everyone, like motor cars and foreign travel.

Criminals are "birched", beaten with bundles of sticks on their bare bottoms until they bleed.

A vociferous minority feel there should be much more of this. You will be expected, at least in conversation, to take sides. If so, try this opening gambit:

"Can't say I go along with you people entirely on this flogging!"

From this position you can fire in all directions. If he says—

"Nor do I, Brash! Down with brutality!"

"How do you feel about flogging?"

—then you will have found a friend. On the other hand he may say—

"Soft, you Americans, soft! Good beating can work wonders! Beaten all through my youth, and look at me! Charactah! Twelve of the best! Only language they understand!"

In this case, try the *you-don't-go-far-enough* approach:

"Don't misunderstand me, Major! Actually I'm a rack and thumbscrew man, myself. You don't go far enough, by half!"

"Well, now, Brash, I wouldn't quite say——"

"Nothing like a good stretching to make a new man of you! Draw and quarter a few lads in Trafalgar Square and see what *that* does to your crimes of violence!"

You will make many friends:

"Good man, Brash. Don't go with him *all* the way, though."

"SHOULD I WAG MY TAIL?"

Wag your tail if you must, but avoid jumping into their laps:

"Buckley, may I present Major William Strathmore-Eakens?"

"Well, hiyah Bill! Howsa boy?"

If you should dare to go this far, you will see mouths fall open, and consternation reign. Only after you have known an Englishmen a long time will he speak to you frankly about this:

"Why not, Nige? Why not call people by their first names, right away? What's wrong with intimacy?"

"Nothing, Buckley—but how can you really be intimate with anyone if you pretend to be with everyone?"

Send your answers to this question to our information center.

HOW TO USE POLITENESS AS A WEAPON

You will find that the British are the most polite people you have ever met. They will be polite to you even if they don't like you. In fact, they will be *especially* polite if they don't like you. They have learned to use politeness as a weapon. Politeness can be fired off either at long or short range. Note the long-ranged, or I-don't-believe-we've ectually-*met* variety:

"I *dew* hope you'll *pardon* me! You *dew* know this is a queue, don't you? Thenk you very *much*!"

This will take little practice. The short-range, or hand-to-hand weapon is more difficult to master, but can be effective:

"Thank you so much for letting me see your *lovely* garden, Mr. Brash! It's *so*, ah, *woodsy*, and *untamed*!"

(Translation: "The place is an absolute jungle. I can count four dead roses that haven't been clipped, and isn't that a weed, in plain sight?")

HOW TO BE RUDE TO YOUR FRIENDS

Here, where politeness is spread so thickly, rudeness has become a badge of intimacy. Once your acquaintances start being rude to you, you will know you have been accepted as a friend:

"Buckley, you'd better sack that bloody gardener. Does he think that weed is a lupin?"

(He is your friend. He is subtly congratulating you on having a "gardener" instead of an itinerant Italian who comes on alternate Wednesdays, and he thinks you've got a fair show, for a Yank.)

LEARN TO LIVE IN THE FUTURE

It is a social error in England to live in the present. All the proper English live at least two months in the future.

"Buckley, the Price-Johnsons want us for cocktails on Sunday, the 23rd."

"Fine, Peg, but the 23rd is a Thursday."

"Not *this* month, *next* month. She was afraid she'd

asked us a bit too late."

Buy a "diary", or small date book. Get it early, by mid-October, or they will all be gone. Carry it everywhere, as the English do. You will consult it almost hourly.

"Telephone for you, Peg. Some joker says she's from the beauty shop—about your Christmas hair-do."

"Oh, dear, I hope I'm not too late!"

"It isn't even November yet!"

"Hello, Miss Clare? . . . No, I'm engaged December 22nd. Can you manage the 23rd?"

Buy your summer clothes in early spring, your Wimbledon tickets before the snow melts, and your Christmas ham before the leaves fall—or they will all be sold. Your thoughts will always be groping into the distant future, and you will forget the date you made two months ago—for tonight.

HOW TO EAT IN ENGLAND

Do not change your table manners. The British will be continually fascinated by the way you keep putting your fork down and picking it up again, first in the left hand, then in the right hand, like a Swiss bell ringer. They will admire you. They will know you can do something they cannot.

Prove to them you *can* do it their way if you want. Hold your fork firmly in your left hand. Point it down, directly at the potatoes. Never let it go. Never shovel! Minor descriptive gestures can be carried out with the fork held tightly in your fist. Food like peas can be troublesome to the novice, but not for long! Plaster them to the back of your fork, with your knife. Mashed potatoes can be helpful here, and they are in fact often served with peas. You will find that any child can do it—but make it clear that you feel the American way is the *polite* way.

The British method was developed because of the boarding school, where eating is done at breath-taking speed. You will need to use the high-speed or fixed-fork method *only if you are living at a school*. There will be no time to shift the fork from hand to hand. Putting the fork down for a fraction of a second can result in plates being snatched away, with the food uneaten.

Americans living at Oxford or Cambridge (where a four-course meal has been served and partly eaten in as little as 11½ minutes) have approached starvation, and have only survived by switching to the quick-firing British style.

"WILL I *WANT* TO EAT IN ENGLAND?"

Yes, you will, after the first few days. It is not as bad as everyone says. Little by little, the English are learning to cook. You will think they over-cook everything, and they will think you under-cook everything, so you will be even.

You will not starve. In fact, you will probably gain twenty pounds in the first six months. The British eat six times a day, at breakfast, elevenses, dinner, tea, supper, and a snack before bed. And they eat carbohydrates *with* their carbohydrates:

"What'd you have for lunch at Ian's, Pete?"

"Baked beans on toast, French-fried potatoes, boiled potatoes, noodles, and cake with custard on it. It was smashing!"

They eat cookies, candy, meat pies that are almost all pastry, sandwiches that are 98% bread, sausage rolls, scones, crumpets, and two or three kinds of potatoes with every meal. They pour custard on everything that is sweet, and bottled sauce, like Worcestershire or A1, on everything that is not.

While you are bursting your buttons, you will see all around you lean faces and flat stomachs. No one knows why. Some say it is all the shivering that uses up the calories. Make your own investigations:

"And after the eighteen holes you played *tennis*, Nige?"

"The girls needed a fourth for mixed doubles, Buckley. Just five or six sets."

"And three hours of gardening?"

"Had to clean up a few odds and ends."

Once you set up your own kitchen you will be able to eat beautifully, and for less money than you ever did in the States. You can buy the best beef and lamb you have ever eaten, fine British cheeses, like Cheddar, Cheshire, and Stilton, and good fruits and vegetables. Good hams and bacon come in from Denmark, and wines and cheeses from the continent.

Your children, of course, will have their own ideas:

"But Buckley, all Pete and Ted want are bangers and mash, pork pies and custard!"

(Translation: "bangers and mash": pork sausages and mashed potatoes.)

"CAN THE UPPER CLASSES READ?"

Yes, they can, and without moving their lips. In fact, people read more in Britain than they do in the States.

Everyone reads newspapers, and there is a huge variety of them. Every city in Britain has eight different morning papers—and every other city has the same eight, because papers are national, not local, distributed throughout the British Isles. Your choice can range from *The Times*, more conservative than *The New York Times*, to tabloids like *The Daily Sketch* and *The Daily Mirror*, which make the New York tabloids look tame.

At first you will buy just the Paris editions of *The New York Times*, or *The Herald Tribune*, or the London *Christian Science Monitor*, Soon, however, you may need other information:

"Really, Father, this is shocking!"

"*The New York Times* is, Pete?"

"One skimpy paragraph about the Test Match! And not a word about Trueman's bowling, or Dexter's century!"

BUY A BOOK

In America, books are for putting on coffee tables. In Britain people actually read them. More than fifty new titles are published every day, including almost all the new American books, at about half the American price. Try them. You will be able to read them easily, in spite of the funny spellings. You can get hard-bound books from several different book clubs for four shillings, or 56 cents, a month, and paperbacks are everywhere, just like at home.

GO TO CHURCH

You will surely be able to afford going to church, though new American fund-raisers are making even *that* more expensive than it was before.

There are a few things about British church-going that you should know, however.

You will discover that this is a country which does not believe, as America does, in the separation of Church and State. England has an official State Religion, the Church of England. The ruler has been the head of it ever since Henry VIII. On the coins you can read that the Queen is so "by Grace of God", and is "FID: DEF", or "F.D.", which stand for "Defender of the Faith".

While in England the Queen is head of the Church of England, and its defender, and when she crosses the border into Scotland instantly becomes a Presbyterian, and defender of *that* faith. Happily the two faiths are at peace, and do not have to be defended from each other.

Your children, forbidden by law from saying prayers in American schools, will in Britain have regular classes in "scripture", which they usually call "R.I.", for "religious instruction".

If you are an Episcopalian, you will go to the Church of England, but if you are something else you need not, like the Pilgrims, flee the country. The British have freedom of religion now, and there are churches of all kinds. No matter which one you attend, in winter, you will never have to worry about what to do with your heavy overcoat. You will keep it on.

EMERGENCY CHURCH SERVICES

In England the church performs several services unfamiliar to Americans. For example, its ministers will turn out, like the fire department, if you are troubled with ghosts. They have a regular ceremony for Exorcising, which is quite effective, and, like the National Health, is done without charge. Unlike the National Health, neither you nor the ghost needs to produce a stamped card, nor are there any regular monthly payments.

With the growth of black magic, devil's masses, and other black rites sometimes performed, without official

authorization, in churches and churchyards, after hours, the Church of England has been striking back with Curses, calling down the Wrath of God on the interlopers. The Curses, too, are given without charge, and without paper work. Cursing and Exorcising, in fact, are the only two things that can still be done in England without filling in printed forms.

Recently a Curse that was given publicly was withdrawn privately and then later withdrawn again publicly. Theologians are not entirely certain whether a public curse still "works", i.e., retains curse–potential, until publicly un–cursed, at least without notification of the accursed, or curse–ee. Some Americans feel it is a danger inevitable in socialized cursing.

TURN ON THE TELLY

In America, television is generally regarded as something for the children and the lower classes. If you watch it yourself, you are careful not to let anyone know.

In England, the Best People sometimes turn on the telly. And you can do the same.

Before you turn it on, be sure you pay the £4, or $11.20 to the BBC, plus another £1, or $2.80, if you want to listen to your car radio. This will pay for your TV and radio programs for the year.

There are three television channels in London, BBC–1, and BBC–2, which are trying to improve your mind, and the commercial telly, which is trying to sell you things, just like at home, except that they put all the commercials together in bunches, sometimes five or six of them in a bunch.

You will be used to the kind of TV that you can watch *while you are doing something else.* This will not be true of all BBC–TV programs, especially the late ones. It is difficult to concentrate on a bridge game, or ping–pong, and watch Brecht, or Strindberg, or Henry Moore, or the Royal Ballet at the same time.

"Honestly, Peg, how can the British understand this stuff? Some of it is even over *my* head!"

"Turn it a little louder, Buckley, and keep quiet."

The Third Program, on the radio, goes even farther, and in fact stops at nothing. Do you want Sophocles in the original Greek, or a lecture on ichthyology? Turn it on, and call in the neighbors. It is the class system again, with its insidious doctrine that some people are more intelligent than others. Do not form a taste for this kind of broadcasting, or you will never be able to return home to the healthy democratic system, where every program can be understood by the smallest child.

"WHAT DO I NEED MONEY *FOR*?"

After reading all this, you may wonder, indeed.

However, you will find there are a number of things you will want to do with money. And even if you don't, every red-blooded American will want to make it *for its own sake.*

In just a moment we will show you how.

18

"Do I WANT My Daughter to be a Duchess?"

Part III

LUCKILY for you, your daughter will not be insensitive to the perils that lie around her on every side.

She may even cooperate with you in your efforts to enter her in an American university:

"I've decided I shall take the American College Boards after all, Father."

"Good, Susan."

"I've re-thought the whole thing."

"Let me remind you, Buckley, that Sonny Clemens is going back to Dartmouth next fall, and we have been seeing quite a lot of that Olds-mobile lately."

It is possible, by writing scores of letters, having her take many tests, and going several times to the States, to find your daughter a place in an American university:

"Think we did it, Nige. Got Susan entered at Radcliffe, I think——"

"Funny you should say that, Buckley. My son Ian brought up the subject of American universities, too. Happened to mention Harvard."

"No connection, of course?"

"Couldn't be, Buckley. Ian's much too terrified of Susan. Of *all* girls. Terribly shy."

Your daughter will not be insensitive to the perils that lie around
her on every side.

"Only one hitch to the Radcliffe deal, Nige. No
idea how we can pay for it. With tuition, holidays, and
fares back and forth, it'll come to nearly $5,000 per
year, per kid."

"That's roughly four times what it would cost to
go to Oxford."

So you can see, this *is* one reason you may need
to make—and keep—money in large amounts. Full
instructions on how to do this are just a few chapters
ahead.

19

Ambulances Are for Everyone

"IS ENGLAND REALLY A PEST HOLE?"

DO NOT be afraid.

Nothing can possibly hurt you after you leave America.

Like all Americans bound for Europe, you will be loaded to the ears with shots, pills, and dire warnings. They will squirt you full of cholera, bubonic plague, typhoid, smallpox, and the Black Death. You will think you are going to darkest Africa, or the jungles of the Amazon.

You will be told to boil your water, and your milk, and even to wash your lettuce in chlorine.

All Americans believe Europe is a pest hole, and that you are as infectious as an open wound.

After the first week or so you will discover that Europe, and even England, are almost civilized, have pasteurized milk, water supplies that are as closely inspected as your own, and vegetables with no more germs on them than any others, and considerably less DDT.

However, it is only fair to warn you that in England you will be living under socialized medicine, and every American knows how dangerous that can be.

SET THEIR MINDS AT REST

Regardless of how worried you may be about your own safety, your first mission will be to set at rest the minds of your British friends who plan to travel to America. They have heard such horror stories (printed in the socialist press) about the A.M.A., and American medicine generally, that they fear to visit the States:

"No, no, Nige! Relax! American doctors are the best in the world."

"For the very rich, you mean?"

"For the very poor, too. If you're absolutely bankrupt, or haven't a penny, they won't let you die."

"Friend of mine got sick in New York, had to go to hospital for a month. Nearly ruined him financially."

"Well, yes, of course. Not for the middle classes, Nige. Let's say you just feel kind of lousy, but you can still walk. Go to a drugstore."

"Chemist's shop?"

"That and more, Nige. In the States it's the druggist who gives medical attention to the middle classes—unless they're practically dying."

"He must be very busy."

"He is. Sometimes the actual diagnosis, or treatment, is done by the young fellow in the front, the one who sells the ice cream, and the mineral waters. He remembers what the druggist gave people before. One look at you and he may say, 'Hey, y'ever try ona dese seven way tablets, Mac?'"

"What are they?"

"Say, two for sixty-nine. That's about five shillings."

"What will they do?"

"Pep up your blood, make a new man of you. He can

show you. He's got a moving diagram right there, in colors. Stomach, liver, everything. Scientific. Backed up by TV commercials, full page ads—millions. Fix you up good as new, Nige, till you can get back to the free doctors."

THE DOCTOR IS YOUR FRIEND

In England, where medical care is paid for by taxes, the doctor is your friend. Use him. Whether you do or not, you will still have to pay the same amount every month to the National Health. Doctors, ambulances, and hospitals are free; even false teeth, eye glasses, and prescriptions are almost free.

Has your main concern been that sickness could bankrupt you? Set your mind at rest! In England you will have no worries at all, except to find the doctor:

"Oh, Buckley, I think Ted has a strep throat, or something."

"Get out the old Health Card, Peg! Phone up the Doc. Let's sample this free medicine. Tell him to pop over, we'll be in all evening."

"I called his number. The nurse said the surgery opens at six, doors open at five-thirty."

"I'll pop over there with him. Shouldn't take a minute."

You will decide it is silly to get there at 5:30 if nothing happens until six. When you arrive, at 5:50, there will be seventeen patients in the waiting room, sitting absolutely still. You and your child will sit beside them. No one will move until a bell rings, at 6:15, when the first patient will go into the surgery. You will time him at 18 minutes 32 seconds, and will ask the patient next to you:

"Can you tell me how many doctors there are?"

"Ah, pardon me."

"Oh!" *(She will jump. It will be the first word anyone has spoken.)*

"Can you tell me how many doctors there are?"

"One."

You will note that the temperature in the waiting room is about 45. You will find an old comic book and try reading it to your child until he goes to sleep. You will attempt to multiply 18½ by 17, in your head, will wonder if you should go home and have dinner, and will note that eight more patients have come in after you.

At 7:47, with nine patients still ahead of you, you will rise quietly, carry your little boy out with you, and telephone a friend:

"You can always be a *private* patient, Buckley—of any doctor except your own National Health doctor. Very expensive, though."

Once you are a private patient, you will not have to spend all that time waiting in the surgery. You will go right in.

BE DESPERATE

If you cannot afford the private patient fees, and want to avoid all that waiting, do as the British do: be desperate.

"Oh, Buckley, while you were gone, I sent your Pete off to the hospital. Fell off his bike. Leg bleeding."

"Oh, no, Nige!"

"Not to worry. Ambulance came right around."

"An *ambulance*?"

You will be terrified. You know that in the States no one calls an ambulance unless the patient is dying. A ride in an American ambulance costs almost as much as buying a small family car.

"Told them he might bleed to death. Only way, Buckley. Might take days otherwise. Absolutely free, too, not like taxis."

You will rush to the hospital. On your way in you will see other ambulances arrive, most of them like minibuses, with people sitting in them, and jumping out when they arrive. In England, ambulances are for everyone.

"I want to get him home right away, Buckley!"

"The doctor said he might have to stay a week, Peg."

"But he's just a little boy!"

"You can see him again on Tuesday, between three and five."

You will find it is almost as hard to get anyone *out* of a hospital as it is (barring emergencies) to get him in:

"Nine days, Buckley, and they won't let me have him back!"

"Poor kid!"

"Well, there are fifteen other kids in the ward. They're watching TV, and having a ball."

Once you do get anyone out, he'll be as good as new, and no one will mention money at all.

"WILL I SURVIVE?"

No one knows why, but most Americans do survive their stay in Britain. Some say it is because they are tempted to exercise by the legions of running and jumping Englishmen all around them, and because they get all that fresh air, even indoors.

But survival alone, as we shall see, is not enough.

20

How to be Ruled

IF YOU ARE an alien living in England you will not have to worry about choosing your leaders. It will all be done for you. Like an Englishman living in America, you will have taxation without representation.

All you have to do to be represented is to go back home.

"DOES IT REALLY MATTER TO ME?"

You have been brought up in a country where it is almost impossible to tell one political party from another. "Is it," you will ask, "the same in England? Does it matter which party gets in?"

In England it *does* matter. And your British friends will really suffer over politics:

"Why worry about it so much, Nige?"

"Don't *you* worry about American elections, Buckley?"

"Why? Both our parties stand for everything. Have to. Got little men with questionnaires. Same as for the flavor of a toothpaste. Find out just what you want and promise to give it to you."

"Democrats *are* left of Republicans, aren't they?"

"Except in the South, where they're right of everybody."

"Confusing. No doubt in England which party is right and which is left. And it makes a hell of a difference which one gets in."

You will never really understand British politics, but you will need a few simple facts to get you through dinner table conversations.

"WILL I EVER MEET THE RULING CLASS"

This is impossible to define in Britain, but if you mean the Members of Parliament, you may meet them anywhere. You have probably never chatted socially with a real, live Congressman, but you may find yourself eating dinner with an M.P. without even knowing it.

HOW TO TELL M.P.'s FROM PEOPLE

There are several easy ways to spot members of Parliament:

1. He will have an unsettled look,

like a person in the midst of a game of musical chairs. This is because in Parliament there are not enough chairs to go around. In fact there aren't any chairs at all, only benches. He doesn't have a desk, a locker for his hat, or a place to put his briefcase.

Comfort him and put him at his ease. Let him know you are his friend. Make him understand you wish he did have a place to sit down.

2. He will look as though he is doing two things at once

He is. In Britain, law-making is regarded as a spare-time job. M.P.'s are not paid enough to live on, so they are always given the morning off, to do something else to help pay the bills.

—or a place to put his briefcase.

If he does become Prime Minister, or a member of the cabinet, he may have to give up his regular job, but he will still be doing two things at once, because all cabinet members are M.P.'s, too. He will be making the laws in the afternoon, and enforcing them the next morning.

Do whatever you can to soothe his nerves and ease his burden. Do not mention the latest public opinion polls, or discuss the budget. Talk to him softly about gardens and dogs.

3. "Can I tell his party from his face?"

Yes, even if you could never tell a Democrat from a Republican. After watching British TV for a few months, it will be easy to separate Labour party members from Conservatives. Conservative members look like managing directors, and many of them are. Labour members look like union officials, or professors. There is no use trying to pick out Liberal members, who can look like anybody; but at the moment there are so few of them that they are hard to find.

HOW TO BE A PRIME MINISTER

Do not try, yourself, to become Prime Minister.

"Is it," you may say, "against the Constitution?"

No, not exactly, because there isn't any British Constitution, just rules written on bits of paper, here and there, or handed down in song or story. But most people believe it is probably not possible for an American citizen to become Prime Minister, though it seems to be comparatively easy for an American woman to become the *mother* of one. Some of the best Prime Ministers have American mothers. Though it is too late for your wife to try, it will be something for your daughter to think about.

However, for Englishmen it is far easier than you think.

In Britain you do not need to have the Father or Hero Image so essential to becoming an American President. You will not have to appeal to twenty-five million voters. The Prime Minister is not chosen by the people. The people have practically nothing to do with it. The only voters who elect him are the members of his own constituency, which may consist of a few farms, where he doesn't even have to live, and where he has virtually no chance of losing. He may be elected by fewer people than elect a county sheriff in Indiana.

YOU DO NOT HAVE TO SMILE

If you recall the last half dozen presidential elections in America, and all the elections since television, you will note that it was always the man with the bigger smile who won.

This is not true in Britain at all. You can be elected Prime Minister without smiling *once.*

In fact, to be Prime Minister all you have to do is to be chosen by the *other* members of Parliament, and they do not mind whether you smile at them or not.

HOW TO HELP YOUR LAWYER HELP YOU

In England the laws are lying around everywhere, and sometimes it takes weeks to find them.

Remember this the first time you get a bill from a lawyer:

"Peg! Look at this! Two hundred pounds! Just for looking over a contract!"

"My, Buckley, that's over five hundred dollars!"

"He didn't even *do* anything. Well, we won't go to *him* any more!"

At first you will change lawyers every time you get a bill. The new one will always charge you just as much:

"Why, Nige, why?"

"It's all based on a fixed percentage, Buckley. In this case, the value of your house."

You will understand how the Englishman feels about American doctors. In Britain the man of medium income cannot afford to go to court. It is only for the rich. It can even be financially ruinous to be innocent. You could be accused, by mistake, of manslaughter, judged innocent, and be acquitted—and still have to pay legal costs high enough to bankrupt you.

There are two other things you should know about British lawyers:

1. If you are going to court, you must have *two* lawyers, never one. You will go to a solicitor, who then goes to a barrister. A solicitor is not allowed to present cases in any major court. The barrister is the one you have seen in the movies with the funny wig. Barristers speak only to solicitors, so you cannot go directly to him. You cannot have a barrister without having a solicitor first.

2. There are no law schools in the American sense, as part of universities, though it is possible to "read law" at Oxford or Cambridge. Law students spend a sort of apprenticeship at the Inns of Court. It is something like being an intern in a hospital.

Even if you have not run foul of the law, you will by this time be in serious need of money.

Luckily this is a problem that can be solved quickly, and we shall get at it straightaway.

21

How to Get Rich in England

Part II

DEEP IN THE HEART OF TAXES

ONCE you have reached the top of the ladder as a salaried man in England, you will discover you are going farther into debt every year. This will be on account of taxes. Great Britain is the most heavily taxed country in the world.

There will be no point in working any harder to make a higher salary. It will all be taken in income tax. For a married man this is about twice as high as it is in the States.

None of your other taxes (such as the real estate tax, or "rates") is deductible from your income tax, so you will be paying taxes *on* your taxes.

MAKE IT A CAPITAL GAIN

The only way to get rich in England is to make it a capital gain.

In America, "making it a capital gain" has long been regarded as a license to steal, because capital gains are taxed at a maximum of 25%.

In England there is *no capital gains tax at all* (except for a few technical kinds of short-term trading). Though a salaried man will have almost every penny over £10,000 a year ($28,000) taken away in income tax, you can make a cool million a year in capital gains and pay not one penny.

A few moments' thought may be rewarding:

"Wonderful site for the new plant, sir."

"Glad you like it, Bash."

"Just wondering if we should make a dicker for a few hundred acres more, across the road."

"Wouldn't want to commit the company on any *more* land, Bash."

"No need to trouble the Board, sir. I was thinking—how about just you and me, sir, on a *personal* basis. Few hundred pounds would get an option on the land—if we do it before the news gets out, that is. Make a beautiful shopping center for the employees, wouldn't it, sir?"

"Where the hell would we get the capital to build it Bash?"

"Build it or not, as we please, sir. Once the word about the plant gets out, we could make fifty thousand just re-selling the land. Or any British insurance company would jump at putting up the money to build. After we lease all the shops we could sell the whole thing for twice the cost."

Just a few days' work getting a few signatures here and there, and you can make more, after taxes, than you made in years of dreary work. You will wonder why you hadn't thought of it before.

"Free and clear, Bash? Not a penny of tax?"

"Wouldn't do to tax that sort of thing, sir. Bound to stifle initiative. It's the sneaky professional man they're after."

THE THINKING HAS ALL BEEN DONE FOR YOU

Once you have a good chunk of capital to play with, you will find it takes little thought to make more. No need to be creative. The thinking has all been done for you. Just do anything that worked four or five years ago in the States:

"How do you *know* soft ice cream and drive-ins will work here, Bash? They're un-British!"

"Exactly what they said about hamburger stands, super markets, Coca-Cola, juke boxes, tenpin bowling, and bingo. It's more than money! It's spreading a way of life."

You will be stimulating enterprise, reducing unemployment, and scattering wealth to everyone, including yourself.

Soon you will be in a position to live like a lord. Even, in fact, like a Duke.

You will feel, for a while, that you are surely on an unassailable pinnacle, and that problems can never touch you.

Remember, however, that in England, money isn't everything, and that victory does not always go to the owner of the fattest purse.

22

"Should We Grind the Faces of the Poor?"

IS THERE REALLY A CASTE SYSTEM?

FROM the moment a porter at the airfield takes your bags you will know the British have a caste system.

You will see by the way he touches his cap and calls you "Sir" and acts as though you were a thing apart.

The whole time you are in England it will be all around you. Every American says it is a bad thing, and so will you. You will think it is not democratic:

"Disgusting, isn't it, Peg?"

"Undemocratic."

"All men created equal, and all that."

"Definitely, Buckley. I keep remembering how equal that cleaning woman was, the one we used to have once a week, on Long Island. I had to go meet her at the train, have her breakfast waiting for her, and serve lunch to her. She complained if the lunch wasn't good enough."

"She knew she was just as good as we were."

"Better. She used to scold me."

"Compare that with this daily cleaning woman here. 'Madam' this, 'Sir' that. Rides her own bicycle. Knocks before entering a room. Does exactly what she's told. Disgusting, isn't it?"

"Degrading, Buckley."

You will wonder how long you can bear up under this system. "Is it," you may ask, "bigger than we are?"

"SHOULD WE SET THEM ALL FREE?"

Your first reaction will be to set them all free, and your first opportunity will come when you go into business for yourself and have a job of work to do. Let us say you have bought some land, and have hired a group of workmen to clear it for you.

"You're on your own now, men. It's up to you. Understand everything?"

"Oh, yes, guv'nor, thank you, sir."

"All clear about the back end, too?"

"Don't fret about that, sir. We'll do the lot!"

You will try to fight off a warm, sticky, and lordly feeling, as though someone has been licking your hand, and resolve once again to set them all free.

You will come back a few hours later to see how well they have finished the job, and will find the men sitting around drinking tea:

"What's the matter here?"

"Oh, so glad you could come, sir."

"You haven't done anything at all."

"Didn't want to go any further without asking your opinion about the pipe, sir. What is your decision about that, sir?"

"Why didn't you phone me?"

"Didn't want to disturb you, sir."

It will all be done with the greatest respect and humility. This may cool your fire a bit, but will not

As though someone had been licking your hand.

basically dampen your resolve. You may speak to your English friends about it:

"Where did I go wrong, Nige?"

"You have been a sitting duck, Buckley. You have been shot, plucked, roasted, and eaten. You cannot deal with them like that."

"Feudalism is dead, Nige!"

"You know it, and I do, but they are so used to being the lower classes that they are expert at taking advantage of it. It's a skill they have developed over many generations."

"IS THERE A WAY OUT?"

Do not give up!

Many Americans have come face-to-face with this problem. No one has ever completely solved it. Go on being as lovable as you can, meanwhile taking full advantage of the caste system without assuming any responsibility for it.

Always take the position that there are no classes, and that you are slightly on top of all of them.

Your house may become, like London's new hamburger stands, an oasis of classlessness.

"Well, Buckley, I'll bet that's the first time Mrs. Payne-Warrener ever sat down to tea with Mrs. Tibbitts."

"Seemed to go all right."

"How can you tell?"

You will never be really sure.

23

"Is it Time to Leave?"

ARE YOU GOING NATIVE?

So MANY Americans ask: "How long should I be an expatriate? Am I beginning to lose touch? Have I started to cross over?"

The first danger sign will be when a new American asks you:

"Well, uh, Mr. Brash, are you English—or American?"

This is a mistake the British will not make for some time. However, you will begin to wonder. "Am I," you will ask, "beginning to go native?"

There are a number of tests you can perform to determine just how native you are going.

MAKE THE CHILD-LANGUAGE TEST

One good measuring stick is the language (or actually, languages) of your children.

First they will become bilingual. They will speak to you in pure Wagon Train, or Perry Mason (from the daily American lessons on the Telly) and then will swing around to the telephone and talk to a British school-mate in a language you will refer to as clipped-nothing, and of which you will understand only an occasional word.

The second stage will come when they stop talking American to *you*:

"Oh, father, I got into such a flap because we're breaking up that I left my Mac in Jennifer's boot!"

"You—what?"

(She will mean simply that she got excited because the school term was over and left her raincoat in the trunk of someone's car.)

(Serious students will find an entire chapter about the British Language and How to Understand It in the APPENDIX.)

The third and final stage will come when you don't notice they are talking British to you, and when you start talking it back to them.

There are some who say this is the time to leave.

MAKE THE EASY "QUEEN" TEST

Another test you can make to determine how native you are going is *The Anthem Test*, or *The Four Stages of "The Queen"*.

You will discover quickly that at most public gatherings the national anthem, or "God Save the Queen" is played. Everyone is expected to stand more or less at attention until it is over. It is sometimes referred to in the program simply as "The Queen".

You will go through various emotional stages about "The Queen", and together they form a good barometer of how–native –you–are–going.

First Stage: You will think they are playing "My Country 'Tis of Thee", and will wonder how they knew you were here.

Second Stage: You will know it *is* "God Save the Queen" and you will have that dear-Motherland feeling, and will be quite choked up. You will stand at rigid attention, and will have just the trace of a tear in your eye.

Third Stage: You will have moved to the suburbs and will attend the local cinema, the other one that has not yet been converted into an American bowling alley. As the picture ends and the lights come up, one of you may forget, and say:

"Let's go, Buckley."

"Steady on, girl! Remember 'The Queen'."

"Of course!"

An almost unrecognizable recording of The Anthem will be played, sometimes accompanied by a picture of the Queen. You will stand at rigid attention, though you may no longer have a tear in your eye. But you will be the only ones who are, except for a retired colonel of advanced age, and two boy scouts.

The rest of the audience, who knew it was coming, are already ducking out the front exit, to the parking lot. The local rule is: if you are actually at your seat, because your wife can't find her other shoe, stand and face it. If you are already in motion, don't stop.

Fourth Stage: You will join the rest of them, ducking for the parking lot.

When this stage arrives you will know it is time to leave England.

MAKE THE "AM-I-EDUCATED?" TEST

Another easy gauge is the education test. Do you feel more or less educated than the British? Superior or inferior? This feeling will change, back and forth, and can be divided into well-defined stages:

First, or Bitter Inferiority Stage: You will be overwhelmed, at first, by the way the English talk.

"But, gosh, Peg, they all talk like—like———"

"Like *professors*, that's how, Buckley."

"They must all be mental giants!"

After a short while you will realize this it not actually true. The English do not talk like professors; it is American professors who talk like the English. In fact, they sometimes manage this after an eight-week visit; a year's exchange at Oxford can make them completely unintelligible, even to the British.

Second, or Am-I-An-Egghead Stage: Shortly afterward you will be struck by an irresistible feeling of intellectual superiority:

"You know, Peg, I think we're the only ones at that party who went to a university!"

"I was certainly the only *woman* who had, Buckley."

This may be literally true, as far as it goes.

Third, or Galloping-Sixth-Form Stage: You will continue to feel unbearably superior until your children enter the Sixth Form at school. This is the last two or three years of pre-university schooling, and is taken at the ages of about 16 through 18, when Americans are finishing High School. They will begin to specialize sharply, and their homework will be stimulating to everyone:

"Uh, I'm afraid that's beyond me Susan."

"I thought you went to a *university*, Daddy."

You may discover they are studying things you had in your sophomore or junior year at the university, and some things you never had at all.

After weighing all these factors, you may discover that you are still not sure whether it is time to leave England.

You may even find that the decision is not entirely up to you—as we shall see in the next chapter.

24

"Do I WANT My Daughter to be a Duchess?"

Part IV

IF YOUR daughter is of a romantic age, you may find that you will not have to worry about any of the other reasons for staying in England—or leaving.

She will give you enough reasons, all by herself.

"I thought Susan was all set to go back to the States to college, Peg."

"More important now than ever, Buckley."

"Well, she was just saying this morning that she couldn't *stand* being so far away from us."

"Let me remind you, Buckley, that I saw her twice today on the back end of a motorcycle, and once on a scooter. And yesterday she asked me a guarded question about bridesmaids—in *England*. Do you realize that our daughter may become the wife of a European *peasant*?"

Luckily for you, however, the parent—and especially the father—has full authority in England. It is not like the loose arrangement common in the States, where young people flout parental control. Your role will be recognized by everyone. Do not abuse this power:

"Nige, have *you* seen Susan? I told her not to go running off."

"No, Buckley. I told Ian the same thing, and I can't find him, either."

"She couldn't be with *him*, could she, Nige?"

"Not likely, old boy. Ian's terrified of her. I've done *my* best to get them together. After your money, you know. Afraid he's much too shy."

"She must be off on those motorcycles again. Only one thing will save us now, Nige. Pull up stakes. Sell the house. Get out of England!"

Once you have made up your mind, clearly and strongly, to leave England, nothing can stop you:

"Well, Peg, it's all done! House sold!"

"Oh, dear, and after all that work."

"Well, with Susan at this dangerous age, it's the only thing to do."

But there are always little surprises for every father and mother:

"Father, before you finish *all* that packing——"

"It *is* finished, Susan."

"Well, I thought I ought to tell you—Ian and I have just decided to get married."

"Nigel's Ian? Next door?"

"You have to realize, Father, that some of the *nicest* people in England don't have titles at all, and——"

"He's been going after you, behind my back?"

"Not entirely, Father."

"*You* went after *him*?"

"Well, actually, when a boy is as shy as Ian, what else can a girl do?"

Try to buy your next English house not *too* far from where they will live. The second time around you will find it is far easier to do the central heating, the woodworm, the plumbing, and the electricity. It will not be cheaper, but it will be easier.

"Bad enough having a Yank in the family, Buckley, without having another sloppy garden——"

"Glad to have you give us a hand, Nige."

"Can't do much more than supervise, old boy. Been up the last few nights with my *lumbricus*."

You will be ready, once more, to settle down to the carefree, effortless life of the British aristocrat. Indeed, once you have learned how to live like a Lord, you will find it is difficult to stop.

L'Envoie

JOIN hands with us now as we say good-bye (or hello, as the case may be) to these lovely islands and the gentle islanders who live upon them.

Listen with us for the far-off rolling of the drums, and rise to your feet beside us, as the strains of "God Save the Queen" fill this damp but fragrant air.

Stand quietly, and allow one tear to roll down your cheek. You will not be expected to sing the words. In fact, no one will mind if you let your thoughts wander, briefly, to other shores, and no one will care if you repeat softly, to yourself, in time with the music:

"My country 'tis of thee,
Sweet land of liberty,
Of thee I sing!"

Appendix

Sex in Britain

SHOULD SEX BE IN THE APPENDIX?

A MATTER of semantics should be straightened out here. We are not referring to the vermiform appendix, which has little to do with sex. However, in these days of universal tolerance, we do not intend to be prudish about this. Anyone who is appendix-oriented will receive no censure from us, as long as whatever is done is done between consenting adults.

We have placed these remarks in the back of the book where they can be removed easily, and hidden from young and prying eyes.

ARE THE BRITISH HOT OR COLD?

Up until last year it was assumed that the British, who are cold to the touch, were sexually frigid. Then, with the sudden blossoming of world-wide interest in the sex lives of the British upper classes, everyone began asking: Is this just the class system at work again? Does this apply only to the hot-blooded aristocrats—or to everybody?

Let us look about us. Stand almost anywhere in Britain and you will see, on all sides, extraordinary numbers of attractive people. There is something for everyone!

Your wife, noting the hordes of tall, straight guardsmen, and the lordly looking Savile Row dandies, will be in a continual state of pitty-pat.

You, too, will be perpetually beside yourself, surrounded by pink, radiant English beauties, with a high percentage of indescribably lovely blondes.

You will wonder how the British manage to resist each other—and, in fact, whether they do.

It is a large question, and one that demands careful study.

"DO ENGLISH SCHOOLS CREATE SEX MADNESS?"

Some believe that the school system is responsible for the fact that the English are sexually disturbed.

Almost all education in England is mono-sexual, with boys and girls strictly segregated. Even Oxford and Cambridge students are not considered mature enough to stand the proximity of the opposite sex. Women at both universities are walled and barred apart in separate colleges, like nunneries, where no ill can befall them, whether they want it to or not.

From earliest childhood the sexes meet only in abrupt and well-chaperoned clashes at holiday time.

Naturally, with this celibate background, the British male is as startled and over-excited by females as the Victorians were by ankles, when they were hidden from public view.

On being confronted by women, socially, he tends to babble in a pretty excess of gallantry to cover his retreat to the safety of his fellows. He will then stand with them in a closely-knit conversational group, discussing cricket. He knows no woman dares follow him this far.

CLUBS ARE FOR HIDING

In Muslim countries women are kept behind walls, where only one man can get at them.

In England men keep themselves behind walls where no woman can get at them. The walls are called Clubs, and the British male knows that once inside he is safe. No woman can enter.

It is regarded by many as part of the sinister American influence that a few clubs have allowed women to enter certain rooms, at limited times. This breach in the wall is not expected to become much wider.

BEWARE THE LONELY WIFE!

Many American males, lovable by nature, and accustomed since childhood to the company of the opposite sex, create an impression they surely do not intend.

You cannot be too careful. Lonely wives, shut out by hostile clubs, can misinterpret simple friendliness and exaggerate a kindly word.

"But, dear——" you may try to explain to your wife, later, "all I did was *talk* to her!"

Make sure your intentions are honorable, and that they are clear to everyone.

BEWARE THE SAVILE ROW SUIT

There are pitfalls, too, for the American woman. Are you used to men dressed in the Ivy League Slouch? Have your loved ones always been shoulderless and slumping, looking like a wet raincoat hung on a peg?

Then beware of the Savile Row suit! British tailors, the most skilful in the world, can make a round-shouldered, pot-bellied, bow-legged pipsqueak into a veritable Mr. Universe. True, the percentage of round-shouldered, pot-bellied, bow-legged pipsqueaks is no higher (and may well be lower!) in England than in America, but in England you cannot tell until the clothes come off. And then, as every woman knows, it is too late.

Trick him into a swim suit (called "bathing costume") before you cross the point of no return.

Remember! The well-tailored Englishman is not always what he seems!

In England you cannot tell until the clothes come off.

ARE THE WOMEN REALLY ON FIRE?

You will find, as an American male, that the women are not merely lonely, on occasion, and unbearably attractive—but also, in winter, will seem to be literally on fire. The skin area most visible, the legs, will be bright red, so bright that it will shine clearly through their nylons.

You, as an alien, will assume they are red all over, and therefore burning with uncontrollable flames. A few of our countrymen, mastering their native shyness, as well as overcoming the traditional British reserve, have discovered that the curious legular blush does often go above the knees, but usually not *far* above them.

The phenomenon is wholly the result of the British practice of people-barbecue, sitting with the legs in a medium-broil position in front of an electric "fire", or heater, or close to a gas or coal fire. This maintains body heat without raising room temperature, and gives the legs a red color which disappears entirely in summer, with no resulting loss in sexual desire.

THE PROOF IS IN THE PUDDING

Or, actually, the bed.

We asked, earlier in this chapter, how the British managed to resist each other. After examining all the evidence, it is clear that (in spite of their inhibitions) they do not.

There is adequate statistical proof that the British are, sexually, the hottest people on earth.

British babies are being born continually, and it is a commonly accepted fact that at least one in five British brides is already pregnant.

All this is in the face of conditions that would drive a rabbit to a nunnery. To quote a recent account in London's *Daily Telegraph*:

"British beds are notoriously damp ... On a typically damp winter's night in Britain the bedclothes of a normal double bed could be found to hold from 3 to 3½ pints of moisture. If we could simultaneously wring out all the moisture present in the bedding of 30 million British beds, the moisture so obtained would keep a city the size of Coventry supplied with water for two days."

The article was about a newfangled kind of electric blanket which goes over the sleeper, a concept revolutionary in Britain. It continued:

"It took 47 minutes for the overblanket to heat up from a cold bedroom temperature of 46 F. to a comfortable 70 degrees."

Sit down and think, for a moment, about that 46 degree temperature, and those 3 pints of moisture. You will realize that the British sexual urge can overcome anything.

What will happen when heated bedrooms and electric blankets become widespread is terrible to contemplate.

THE FLAVOR OF SEX IS CHOCOLATE

England is the only country in the world with flavored sex.

The flavor of sex is chocolate.

The newspaper advertisements, the billboards, and the commercial telly all say that you can drive women mad with desire. Do you need to be handsome, charming, or rich? No. All you need is a box of chocolates costing three and six—or fifty cents.

Chocolate, in England, is an aphrodisiac.

Every American imagines what goes on in British bedrooms:

"Oh, darling, darling! Don't stop! Once more, please!"

"The soft center again, love, or something chewey?"

"I don't care, darling, as long as it's Cadbury's!"

"DO I REALLY NEED TO GO TO PARIS?"

Is it true, as many are beginning to suspect, that Paris is not the only home of ooh-la-la, and that London is not confined entirely to Puritan morality?

Yes, it is. Though the British are second to none in condemning sin, good quality, sturdy British sin is available everywhere, and at prices almost everyone can afford to pay.

Many go to Paris for "le Strip-Tease", but it should be pointed out that there are as many *très hot* ones in London, where it is done with traditional British thoroughness.

"CAN WOMEN BE HIRED IN BRITAIN?"

Yes, they can, but only from themselves. Prostitution is completely legal. A woman can receive men for money without arrest, and without paying protection fees to the police. But soliciting on the street, and living on the proceeds of someone else's prostitution are illegal.

Directories of "models" are available, and card-sized advertisements are sometimes placed in store windows.

SUNDAY IS FOR SIN

In many civilized countries, Sunday morning is reserved for those who wish to go to church, and Sunday afternoons for healthful outdoor activity. This is not the case in Britain, In Britain, Sunday is for sin.

The clean, healthful Sunday pursuits of other countries are not permitted in Britain on Sunday. Football games, tennis tournaments, racing of any kind, in fact, virtually any wholesome public gathering in the open air is forbidden, by unwritten law.

Sunday in Britain is devoted to gardening, and to quiet, dedicated sin.

There isn't anything else to do.

How to Understand British

MANY believe it is easier to cope with a completely foreign language, like French, than with one which seems, on the surface, to be the same, but which actually is not.

The British language, in its written form, will seem to be very much like American, and you will at first be lulled into the belief that the British speak the same language as you.

This, of course, is not the case.

BRITISH IS A LOCAL DIALECT

Try to remember, through it all, that British is a local dialect. You can be sure of this, because the British will understand you, but you will not be able to understand them. They have been hearing your language on the telly, and are sometimes surprised to hear real, live people talk like Perry Mason.

However, you will note that they send their children away to boarding school as soon as they are old enough to turn on the set.

The "British language" you have been hearing on television in the States is not really spoken anywhere. This is a special tongue known as Mid-Atlantic, designed to "sound British" to Americans, and still be understood. The British can understand it, too. They think it is a kind of funny American, and wonder why Robin Hood should talk like a Yank.

ASK THEM TO WRITE IT OUT

If you are desperate to understand something, just ask them to write it out. Carry a pad of paper with you, and pretend you are a little deaf. You will be able to read British easily, in spite of occasional misspellings. Words like "colour" are pronounced "color", almost as we say them, and not "col-oor" as you might expect. It means "color", too. The "u" is silent.

BEWARE OF U-UPPING

Do not remind the British that Shakespeare probably sounded more like an American than like a modern Briton. Ever since Shakespeare's time, the British have been improving the language. They cannot leave it alone. They have been U-Upping it.

U-Upping is hard for Americans to understand. In Britain, language is a status symbol. In America it doesn't matter how you talk; people can tell your status by measuring your car or your swimming pool; you can be very important and still talk like a truck driver. There is no need to U-Up language in America.

In Britain, people tell what class you are in by the way you talk, so naturally language gets more uppity all the time, the way swimming pools in America keep getting bigger.

Words like advantage were U-Upped long ago to "ad-vawn-tage".

A word that is right now in the process of being U-Upped is "privacy", which anyone can tell, by looking in the *Oxford English Dictionary*, is correctly pronounced the way Americans do, with a long "i", or "PRIE-vacy". It is now being U-upped to a short "i", because of the U-Up word "privy", as in Lord Privy Seal. Soon "PRIE-vacy" will disappear, and it will be "priv-acy".

This is going on all the time and you will not be able to stop it.

Everyone knows there are lists of words labelled "U" and "non-U", compiled by a writer named Nancy Mitford. It is "U", standing for university, to say "house", for instance, instead of "home". Ever since the list came out, the British have lived in perpetual fear that they would say a non-U word. Do not worry about this. Even if you learned all the "U" words, it would be impossible to speak Perry Mason and "U" at the same time.

HOW TO SAY THENG-KIOO

The first word you will notice on landing in England is actually two words, though they are said as one. It sounds like "theng-KIOO," and is said continuously by all the natives, the way cats say "meow". Spelled out it reads "Thank you", and the British say it even when it is you who should be thanking them. They say "theng-KIOO" when giving you something, and if you say it back to them, they will try to top you by saying "theng-KIOO verimuch", or even, when pressed, "theng-KIOO verimuch indeed."

The British rarely, if ever, say "thanks", and have no expression corresponding to "you're welcome". In fact, they look strangely at you when you say it. They simply say "theng-KIOO" again.

Some bus conductors say as many as thirty thousand "theng-KIOOs" in one day. Toward evening, it is all right for them to say "Ta", which means the same thing.

HOW TO BE ONE-DERFUL

The British are so modest that they feel it is immoral to use the pronoun "I". "I" is egotistical, and must be avoided at all costs. The costs, of course, are one-manship.

Never refer to oneself as "I", but as "one", as in: "One must watch one's language when speaking to one's wife." Often one becomes so wound up in one's one-ness that one can hardly avoid stepping over one's ones, because, as everyone knows, once one begins one-ing, one must keep on one-ing until one is almost done in.

One-manship not only avoids the use of "I", but gives an air of universality to remarks of the most personal nature. In the statement: "one's underpants have fallen down," the British meaning is, "my own underpants have fallen down", and not, as an American would suspect, that all men's underpants have fallen down.

BEWARE OF BRITISH SLANG

If you are a purist you may be shocked to discover that the British are corrupting our mutual language with slang. This will not only distress you, but will make you wonder what they are talking about:

"Smashing, Brash, smashing! You hit it for six and Bob's your uncle! I bished mine, mucked up the lot. Won't get a tanner for donkey's years!"

"Uh, I beg your pardon?"

You would probably phrase it like this:

"Superb! You achieved the utmost, and are surely in an enviable position, whereas I made a confounded mess of the entire affair, and shall not receive as much as a sixpence in the foreseeable future."

TALK AMERICAN

Your duty as an American is to be a missionary of our way of life, and part of that is our new and easy way of talking, without actually pronouncing words.

The British are already doing research on this, and are now trying to spell out American pronunciations so that, no doubt, they can learn to speak this way, too. A typical experiment in trying to record American speech as it sounds to them might read like this:

"Hey, 'at noo one's a bewdy! Whyuncha Briddish get widdit, like us Murkans, hah? Itsa kinda doody, yeah?"

After you have been in Britain awhile you may find that you are slipping, and the effortless speech of newly arrived Americans may make you quite ashamed. You will see that you are falling into the British habit of pronouncing individual words, in a complicated and time-consuming manner. When you reach this point it may be time for you to return.

SPEAK LOUDLY

Part of the reason why the new American way of talking is becoming so popular in Britain is that it is often spoken loudly, and can easily be heard above other speech, even at impressive distances. You will realize that you, yourself, do not speak louder than the British, but the voices of other Americans ring out clearly.

Americans often use the device of the "overheard remark" as a kind of free U.S. Information Service. After you have lived abroad for some years, you will notice that new Americans are not really talking to each other at all. They are speaking for the benefit of all the people around them.

Some never do drop the habit, and indeed keep it to the very end:

"It's perfectly clear to me, Buckley, that if they'd just use those little shopping carts in the airports, the way we do at home, people wouldn't have to——"

"Easy, now, Peg, easy, girl! Let's leave 'em laughin' when we say good-bye!"

Remember, they mean it in a kindly way. They are trying, ever trying, to right the wrongs and solve the problems they find everywhere. They are pointing out the many ways in which Americans can lead everyone to a better—or at least a more American—world.

The voices of *other* Americans ring out clearly.